Patty Cakes

Patricia Sharrigan

Pacific Press Publishing Association
Boise, Idaho
Oshawa, Ontario, Canada

Edited by Marvin Moore
Designed by Tim Larson
Cover photos by Suzanne Murphy
Inside illustration by Ira Lee
Type set in 12/14 Century Schoolbook

Library of Congress Catalog Card Number: 87-62341

ISBN 0-8163-0762-8

87 88 89 90 91 • 5 4 3 2 1

Dedication

This book is
lovingly dedicated to
my best friend,
my husband,
Paul.

Contents

When-You're-Too-Full-For-Dessert Desserts!

Liquid Sweets

Acknowledgments

I'm pleased to acknowledge the people who helped me create this book and who were a constant source of ideas and support.

Paul Sharrigan, my husband, best friend, toughest critic, and original taste tester. Thanks, Paul, for eating the same desserts time after time until they tasted just right. Thanks for the lovely walks we took while the desserts were in the oven taking form. And most of all, thank you for holding and loving me in the middle of the frustrating and sometimes angry moments when the crust wouldn't flake and the cake wouldn't rise or the cookies crumbled.

Leon and Marijane Portratz, my mom and dad. Thanks, Dad, for pretending you had a sweet tooth. Thanks, Mom, for showing me what it means to have a real love for cooking. Your creativity in preparing every meal we ate taught me more about the art of cooking than any book could have done.

Nancy Cluss, my best friend. Without your encouragement and support, this book would have taken longer to leave my heart and find its way onto paper. Your patience, concern, enthusiasm, and honest criticisms make you a valuable friend.

Mike Farrell. A close family friend. Thank you for letting me prepare the manuscript for this cookbook in your house, and for providing me with a self-correcting Selectric typewriter, endless cups of tea, unlimited use of your pool, and free access to your tape and record collection. These things soothed my body and made the writing of this book much easier. Yet, they would have meant nothing without the time you spent reading the manuscript, your constructive criticism, and most of all, the sincere feelings that you gave so generously.

Josephine and George Jackson, my grandma and grandpa. You were the original whole-grain bakers in my life. I feel your loving spirit every day.

Julie Hollingsworth. Thank you for introducing me to a more nutritious way of living.

Frank Zajaczkowski is a close friend. Thank you for helping me with the rewrite, and for your honesty and tact.

Thank you to all my friends and customers whose praise, as well as criticism, helped make this book a reality.

Foreword

Being a "health-food nut" with a sweet tooth poses an interesting problem—one which for years has kept me searching for the perfect place to eat. In the mid-70s I came upon a wonderful place in Van Nuys, California, called Our Contribution. The name derived, I was told, from the belief that providing pure, nutritious, good-tasting food in a happy atmosphere was, indeed, a contribution.

Well, that was OK with me. And besides, their desserts were fabulous!

Our Contribution became a regular on my beat, until one night I found it had closed. I swallowed hard, and, already missing my favorite desserts, set off in search of a replacement.

Some years later, having searched in vain for a completely satisfying alternative, I was presented with the opportunity to reopen Our Contribution. In no time at all, the deed was done, and I was the owner of what I was more comfortable calling "O.C."

Though it couldn't be called a financial success, my memories of the years at O.C. are filled with warmth and joy—a true sense of having made a contribution, and of mouthwatering meals followed (and sometimes preceded) by a dazzling array of wondrous desserts.

When meeting those who would staff the restaurant, I was introduced to "our baker"—Patricia Sharrigan, a beautiful young woman with a golden aura who had the singular ability to bring light to a dark place simply through the glow of her presence. The joy she derived from her work was so infectious that to this day I can't think of O.C. as separate from her. She became the manager and eventually part owner, but always remained "our baker."

Patricia tantalized our customers with carob cake, carrot cake, raspberry-bottom yogurt pie, corn bread (oh, the corn bread!), cookies, pies, and on and on. More than that, she invested a clear sense of purpose in everything she made—a feeling that whatever she created was a personal gift to the lucky one who ultimately ate it.

So I urge you to read on and bake and create and enjoy. As was the case with Our Contribution's desserts, this book comes, I assure you, from Patricia, "with love."

Mike Farrell
Los Angeles, California

Just Who Is Patty Cakes?

Dear Baker:

I was raised around two very creative kitchens. One belonged to my grandparents and the other to my parents. My mother was never too busy to take the time to make each meal a special occasion. She was as concerned about the *way* food was prepared as she was about *what* it was made from. Maybe she learned that from her mother, for it was in my grandmother's kitchen that I first became enchanted with the smells and flavors of homebaked pies and cakes. Grandma's specialty was her spice cake. I would help her select the spices, butter and flour the cake tins, mix the batter; and together we would delicately trace our initials on the frosted cake.

My memories, curiosity, and sweet tooth led me to take some baking classes. Yet when I began baking my own pies and cakes, they didn't compare to Grandma's. There always seemed to be something missing. I soon realized that many of today's products have been overprocessed and chemically treated, unlike the ingredients Grandma used in her kitchen. In 1975 I began using whole grains and fresh ingredients in all my baking, and the difference in taste was remarkable. Not only did I discover that honey doesn't mean "heavy" and that whole wheat doesn't have to mean "dry," but that it is just as easy to use body-building ingredients as it is to use the artificial, overly processed ones that seem to fill most of today's supermarket shelves. My pies and cakes are light, moist, and full flavored with that wonderful taste that I remember as a child.

When I decided to venture beyond my family and friends, the response was very positive. By 1980 I was head pastry chef for a vegetarian restaurant in Van Nuys, California, called Our Contribution. I began Patty Cakes as part of the restaurant. Since that time, Patty Cakes has become an independent, whole-grain gourmet bakery, specializing in naturally unique baked goods that now sells cakes, pies, muffins, and cookies—and all of them have Grandma in mind.

I think it's important for people to know that there *is* an alternative, healthful option to the many overprocessed, oversweetened, preservative-filled baked goods that are all too available today. Desserts can feed your body instead of taking from it. Desserts can be alive and nourishing.

I want to spark that creative flair that is in all of us so that you will venture beyond the recipes in this book and try out some of your own. All it takes is some curiosity, a willingness to dive in, and a little sense of humor.

I wish I could help each reader with her baking problems right in her own kitchen. Since I can't, I hope that, after reading through *Patty Cakes* and trying its recipes, you'll feel like this book is a friend beside you, a guiding hand to help when your pie doesn't set, your crepe won't flip, or your cake won't come out of its pan..

Have fun! And happy, healthful indulgences to you.

Patricia (Patty) Sharrigan

Beginning Considerations

There are several points I would like to discuss before getting into the actual recipe part of this book that I hope will make your use of the recipes easier. Some readers may be unfamiliar with some of the ingredients that are called for in the recipes. For their benefit, I describe these ingredients here. For those who like to have everything on hand ahead of time, I have listed the utensils that will be needed in order to prepare the recipes in each section. Finally, in this chapter I discuss the various kinds of flours available and how best to store them.

Before You Go to the Market

Several of the ingredients used in the recipes in this book may be unfamiliar to you because you do not normally find at your market. However, a health-food store, or a well-stocked supermarket, can usually accommodate all of your needs. I have prepared a list of the foods that are most likely to be new to you and also a list of recommended items that will help to enhance the flavor of your baked goods.

Agar
Unlike gelatin, which is derived from animal tissue, agar is a gelatinlike substance derived from seaweed. It is used as a thickening agent.

Arrowroot
Arrowroot is a natural starch. It comes from a tropical American plant that has rootlike subterranean stems. These stems grow horizontally and produce a nutritious starch. This can also be used as a thickening agent.

Carob
Carob is not chocolate, so. enjoy carob for what it is: an edible fruit. Its long, dry pod contains hard seeds in a sweet pulp. Even after it has been processed, carob contains high amounts of calcium, phosphorus, potassium, natural protein, some sodium, iron, and its own natural sweetener. You can buy it as a powder, liquid, or solid. The nutritional value of carob compared to chocolate is astonishingly high. Because commercial chocolate is rich in fats, carbohydrates, and large amounts of processed sugar, it can add to stomach disorders and acne.

Date Sugar
Date sugar is processed from dates and is a nice alternative to brown sugar.

Fructose
Fructose is a processed sugar derived from fruit. It has fewer calories than cane sugar and is about twice as sweet.

Pero
Pero is a caffeine-free beverage that makes a nice substitute for coffee.

Sea Salt

Sea Salt is easier to digest and contains many minerals that regular table salt does not have. However, if you are on a low-sodium diet you should be careful of your intake of both. In the following recipes, I suggest a minimum amount of salt. A pleasant alternative to salt is lemon juice. Although it cannot be substituted for salt in my recipes, it is very tasty on vegetables.

Recommendations

Butter

I use only lightly salted butter unless otherwise stated in the recipe.

Eggs

I find that extra-large eggs are the best for baking. Use fresh eggs wherever possible. There is an amazing difference in taste and appearance between a fresh egg and an egg that is many weeks old.

Extracts

Use pure extracts only. It will say "pure" right on the package. Some stores carry nonalcohol extracts. These are excellent and superior in taste.

Fruits

For the most part, I recommend using fresh fruits whenever possible. However, if you need to save on time, canned fruits can be substituted for fresh. Just know that canned goods do not supply the same amount of nutritional value as fresh fruits do. They are also not as tasty. If you do choose to use canned fruits, look for those in unsweetened, low-sugar juices, with no preservatives added.

Honey

Since there are so many different types of honey on the market, there are some things you should know before choosing a particular kind for your baking needs. Every honey has a different taste. Usually the lighter in color, the lighter the taste. Keep this in mind, because your selection of honey will definitely affect the taste of your finished product. I have found that clover honey compliments the desserts in this book, but feel free to experiment. Buy raw, unfiltered honey whenever possible. It has many valuable yeasts and digestive enzymes.

Margarine

Look for natural margarine, available in most health-food stores. It has no preservatives, artificial flavors, or animal products. In my opinion, it is better in taste and quality. You will see the word *natural* right on the package.

Oil

Like honey, there are many different types of oils. For dessert baking, I suggest a light, mild oil such as safflower or sunflower. I also suggest cold pressed as opposed to hydrogenated. Cold pressed is easier for your body to digest and more readily assimilated. It is also higher in essential fatty acids than regular commercial oils.

Vegetables

Fresh vegetables are superior in taste and nutritional value to canned. I recommend that you use them. I also recommend organically grown vegetables if you have access to them.

Utensils

Get your hands involved. Remember how much fun it was making mud pies and sand castles? A tin can for water and an old saucepan to stir up the mud was about all you needed. By the same token, it's not necessary to have your kitchen stocked with the latest electronic equipment. I find it much more fun and rewarding to do things by hand. It sure works up an appetite!

However, if the occasion calls for it, or your sweet tooth can't wait, there is an abundance of time-saving devices on the market these days. It seems like every time I turn around, somebody has come out with another gadget that works quicker and easier. The only two I recommend in this book are an electric blender and a mixer.

Cake-making Utensils
Two 8" round cake tins
Two-cup measuring cup
Two one-cup measuring cups, one for the dry ingredients and one for the liquids
Measuring spoons
Mixing bowls: large, medium, and small
Small saucepan
Stainless steel grater
Medium-size rubber spatula
Electric mixer
Electric blender
Wire whisk
Paring knives: large and small
Cutting board
Wooden toothpicks or a stainless steel cake tester
One bundt pan
One blunt knife (for frosting cakes)

Pie- and Tart-making Utensils
9" or 10" pie plate
Cutting board or flat counter
Wooden rolling pin
Pastry blender or two forks
Mixing bowls: medium and small
One-cup measuring cup
Measuring spoons
Paring knife
Saucepans: medium and small
Medium-size rubber spatula
Medium-size spoon
11" tart pan (preferably with a removable bottom)

Cheesecake making Utensils
10"/11" springform pan. This pan is available at cookware stores. It is a round pan made out of stainless steel that has a pitted bottom and removable sides.
Electric mixer
Electric blender
Paring knife
Two-cup measuring cup
Measuring spoons
Mixing bowls: large and small
Small saucepan
Medium-size rubber spatula
Cutting board or flat counter

Cookie-making Utensils
Two 9" x 13" cookie sheets
Mixing bowls: large, medium, and small

Two, one-cup measuring cups
Measuring spoons
Cutting board
Paring knife
Medium-size rubber spatula
Grater
Medium-size spoon
Electric mixer
Table knife
Medium-size saucepan
Rolling pin
Metal spatula
Cookie cutters

Bread- and Muffin-making Utensils
Muffin tin (large enough for 12 muffins)
Mixing bowls: large and medium
One-cup measuring cup
Measuring spoons
Medium-size rubber spatula
Electric mixer
Paper baking cups
9" x 5" loaf pan
Cutting board
Paring knife

Utensils for Miscellaneous Desserts
Electric mixer
One-cup measuring cup
Measuring spoons
Medium-size rubber spatula
Medium-size saucepan
Medium-size spoon
Large mixing bowl
Eight 4-oz. serving dishes
Paring knife
Blender
8" round omelette or crêpe pan (preferably one made of well-seasoned cast iron)
Cutting board
Paring Knife
9" x 13" cookie sheet
Shallow baking dish

Utensils for Making Liquid Sweets
Small saucepan
One-cup measuring cup
Measuring spoons
Medium-size spoon
Electric mixer (for fresh whipped cream)
Your favorite mug

Flour and More Flour

Throughout this book, I recommend the use of whole-wheat pastry flour. I have found that for a few of the desserts, some cakes and cookies in particular, white flour seems to taste better because of the various extracts and spices used in the recipe. For these desserts, I suggest using *un*bleached white flour because bleached flours are chemically treated and may contain some residues of the chemicals used in the bleaching process. Unbleached white flour, being less refined, has a fresher, more wholesome taste.

Whole-wheat *pastry* flour is ideal for dessert recipes because it contains less gluten, is milled more finely, and has a milder taste than regular whole-wheat flour. For a full, rich, nutty taste, try whole-wheat flour the next time you make bread.

There are many types of flour on the market. If you feel adventurous, you certainly have a lot to choose from. Just remember that each flour has its own distinctive taste, along with certain characteristics that affect the consistency and baking time of your dessert. For example, some flours contain less gluten than others, so you may need to add more baking soda or baking powder, or try mixing it with a bit of whole-wheat pastry flour. Some flours contain more oil than others (soy flour, for instance), so you will need less butter or oil in the recipe. I encourage you to be creative and experiment. I have compiled a list of just some of the flours that are available to you. Happy baking!

Rye Flour

Rye flour contains less gluten than wheat flours and adds a fine texture and moistness.

Cornmeal.

Look for stone-ground cornmeal. It still has its germ and other nutrients. I also find that it tastes far superior.

Buckwheat

Buckwheat flour adds a strong, rich flavor to anything that is made from it. Have you ever had buckwheat pancakes? They are rich and wonderful!

Soy Flour

Soy flour adds a rich, nutty taste to your pastries. It contains a fair amount of natural oil.

Brown-Rice Flour

Brown-rice flour is quite mild, smooth, and sweet tasting.

Barley Flour

Barley flour will add a caky quality to your baked goods.

Storing Your Flour and Spices

Flour will eventually go bad. Once flour has gone bad, even after it has been baked it will have a bitter taste to it. I suggest that if you are not a big flour user, buy your flour in smaller quantities. Many markets now sell in bulk (you can usually save money buying in bulk), or some brands of flour are available in prepackaged 2-lb. bags.

But where should you keep the flour? The corner of a high cupboard is not a good place. Remember that heat rises, and because your oven is probably in use some of the time, the air can get pretty hot up there. If you are lucky enough to have a pantry a good distance away from your oven, keep your flour there. The refrigerator is an excellent place because it is continually cool and dry. Flour needs to breathe, but because it can absorb the smells in your pantry or refrigerator I suggest that you store it in a glass jar with a metal jar lid. An old pickle jar is great—cleaned and dried, of course. Poke several tiny holes in the lid, and keep the lid on tight. You can also store flour in a plain paper bag. Place the flour bag in a plastic bag first and secure it loosely with a rubber band.

Spices won't really go bad. They will just loose their pungent taste. You can usually tell if a spice is old by its color. It will be faded, dull, and have very little aroma. Spices should also be stored in a cool, dry place. Do not keep them out by your oven— it's too hot!

CAKES

Cakes have a way of making people smile. Maybe that's why cakes are used to celebrate special occasions such as birthdays and weddings.

Cakes have also been used as prizes. The word cakewalk *comes from a promenade of Black American origin, in which the couple performing the most intricate dance steps received a cake as their prize.*

Apple Spice Cake

Lots of chunky apples and pungent spices help to make this a special cake, rich in vitamin C and potassium.

1 c. safflower oil
1/2 c. honey
2 eggs
1 tsp. pure vanilla extract
1 1/2 c. fresh, chopped pippin apples (approx. 2 medium-size apples, unpeeled, cored, and chopped into small pieces

2 c. whole-wheat pastry flour
1 1/2 tsp. baking soda
2 tsp. cinnamon
1/2 tsp. allspice
1/4 tsp. cloves
1/4 tsp. sea salt
1/2 c. unsulfured raisins (opt.)
1/2 c. chopped walnuts (opt.)

Preheat oven to 325°

Blend oil, honey, eggs, and vanilla until oil and honey do not separate. Add apples and mix until well coated with batter. In a separate bowl mix together flour, soda, spices, and salt. Add dry ingredients to oil-honey mixture and mix until well blended. Fold in raisins and walnuts last. Pour batter into two round 8" cake tins that are buttered and floured. Bake 40-45 minutes, or until a tooth-pick inserted in center of cake comes out clean. After cake has cooled to room temperature, frost with Cream Cheese Frosting. Store in a covered container in a cool place.

Cream Cheese Frosting
2 1/2 c. cream cheese (room temp.)
1/2 tsp. pure vanilla extract
3/4 c. fructose

Blend together cream cheese and fructose until smooth. Add vanilla and continue to blend until vanilla is evenly mixed in and frosting is smooth and creamy.

Classic Carrot Cake

Lots of fresh carrots, pineapple, and coconut blended with just the right spices make this a truly "classic" carrot cake. This cake is rich in vitamin A, with smaller amounts of potassium, calcium, and phosphorus.

1 c. safflower oil
1 c. honey
4 eggs
2 tsp. pure vanilla extract
3 heaping tbsp. crushed
   pineapple (fresh or unsweetened from the can)
2 c. whole-wheat pastry flour
1/2 c. unsweetened coconut
2 tsp. cinnamon

1 tsp. nutmeg
1/2 tsp. allspice
1 1/2 tsp. baking soda
1/4 tsp. sea salt
2 c. fresh, finely grated
   carrots (do not pack)
1/2 c. chopped walnuts (opt.)
1/2 c. unsulphured raisins
(opt.)

Preheat oven to 325°

Blend oil, honey, eggs, vanilla, and pineapple until honey and oil do not separate. In a separate bowl, mix together dry ingredients. Add dry ingredients to oil-honey mixture and mix until creamy. Fold in carrots and blend until evenly mixed into batter. If using walnuts and/or raisins, add to batter last. Pour batter into two round 8" cake tins that are buttered and floured. Bake for 45-50 minutes, or until a toothpick inserted in center of cake comes out clean. Top of cake will not be firm because of moistness. After cake has cooled to room temperature, frost with Orange Cream Cheese Frosting.

Orange Cream Cheese Frosting
2 1/2 c. cream cheese (room temp.)
2 tsp. pure orange extract
3/4 c. fructose

Blend together cream cheese and fructose until smooth. Add orange extract and continue to beat until smooth and creamy. Store cake in a covered container in a cool place.

Blender Banana Spice Cake

Fun to make! Light and moist with just the right amount of banana and spice. Lots of potassium, with some vitamins A, C, and B-12, plus calcium.

2 1/2 c. whole-wheat pastry flour	2 small bananas (very ripe)
1 tsp. baking powder	2 eggs
1 tsp. baking soda	1/2 c. butter
1 1/2 tsp. cinnamon	1 c. honey
1 tsp. nutmeg	3/4 c. buttermilk
1/2 tsp. cloves	1 c. chopped nuts (opt.)

Preheat oven to 350°

Sift together dry ingredients, making sure that spices, baking powder, and baking soda are evenly mixed in. Set aside. Place bananas, eggs, butter, honey, and buttermilk in a blender and blend until mixture is smooth. (Be sure honey gets mixed in. It may tend to stick to the sides of the blender.) Pour wet ingredients slowly into dry, mixing continually. Blend until smooth and creamy. Fold nuts in last. Pour batter into two round 8" cake tins that are buttered and floured. Bake 35-40 minutes or until a toothpick, when inserted in center of cake, comes out clean. After cake has cooled to room temperature, frost with Banana Cream Frosting.

Banana Cream Frosting
- 2 c. whipping cream
- 2 tbsp. honey
- 1 tsp. pure vanilla extract
- 1 small, firm, ripe banana (sliced into thin rounds)
- 1/2 tsp. nutmeg

Whip cream at high speed in an electric mixer, or vigorously by hand using a wire whisk, until cream starts to thicken. Add honey and extract and continue to whip until cream is thick and stiff. Frost cake as you normally would, putting banana slices between the two layers. Sprinkle nutmeg on top of cake. Keep cake covered, and stored in a refrigerator.

Zucchini Cake

Noted for being both mild and moist, zucchini cake contains vitamins A and C, plus riboflavin, calcium, potassium, and phosphorus.

1 c. safflower oil
1 c. honey
4 eggs
2 tsp. pure vanilla extract
2 1/4 c. whole-wheat pastry flour
2 tsp. cinnamon

1 tsp. nutmeg
1/2 tsp. allspice
1 1/2 tsp. baking soda
2 c. fresh, finely grated zucchini (approx. 1 large or 2 small. Do not pack.)

Preheat oven to 325°

Blend oil, honey, eggs, and vanilla until oil and honey do not separate. In a separate bowl sift together flour, spices, and baking soda. Add dry ingredients to oil-honey mixture and mix until smooth and creamy. Fold in zucchini and mix until just moistened by batter. Pour batter into two round 8" cake tins that are buttered and floured. Bake 40-45 minutes, or until a toothpick, when inserted in center of cake, comes out clean. Please note that top of cake will not be firm because of its moistness. Top with Cream Cheese Frosting after cake has cooled to room temperature.

Cream Cheese Frosting
2 1/2 c. cream cheese (room temp.)
3/4 c. fructose
2 tsp. pure vanilla extract

Blend cream cheese and fructose until smooth. Add vanilla and continue to blend until vanilla is evenly blended in and frosting is smooth and creamy. Store cake in a covered container.

"Not So Ordinary" Carob Cake

Even the chocolate lovers who came into the restaurant found this cake a special treat. The combination of oil, buttermilk, and a hint of carob mixed with cinnamon makes this a special cake that is not heavy. Carob contains calcium, phosphorus, natural protein, and some iron.

1 c. oil	2 c. whole-wheat pastry flour
1 c. buttermilk	2 tsp. cinnamon
1 c. honey	1 tsp. baking powder
2 eggs	1 tsp. baking soda
2 tsp. pure vanilla extract	1/2 tsp. sea salt
1/3 c. unsweetened, roasted carob powder	

Preheat oven to 350°

Blend oil, buttermilk, eggs, vanilla, and honey. In a separate bowl sift together flour, carob powder, cinnamon, baking soda, baking powder, and salt. Add dry ingredients to wet and blend batter until creamy. Pour batter into two round 8" cake tins that are buttered and floured. Bake 30-35 minutes or until center of cake springs back when lightly touched with finger and a toothpick inserted in center of cake comes out clean. Frost with Carob Cream Frosting.

Carob Cream Frosting
2 1/2 c. cream cheese (room temp.)
3/4 c. fructose
2 tbsp. unsweetened, roasted carob powder
1 tsp. pure vanilla extract

Blend together cream cheese and fructose until smooth and creamy. Add carob powder and vanilla and continue to blend until frosting is creamy. Frost cake after it has cooled to room temperature. Store in a covered container.

Variations on Carob Cake

Follow these instructions to create variations on the basic carob cake recipe on the previous page. Use the same frosting.

Carob Coconut Cake
Add 1/2 c. unsweetened grated coconut to the dry ingredients after they have been sifted.

Carob Mint Cake
Add 1 1/2 tsp. pure spearmint or peppermint extract instead of the vanilla extract.

Carob Nut Cake
Add 1 c. chopped nuts. Pecans or walnuts are good, but hazelnuts or macadamia nuts are my favorite. Fold the nuts into the batter along with the carob chips.

Peanut-Butter Carob Cake
Add 3 tbsp. old fashioned (nonhydrogenated) peanut butter with the oil drained out, and mix it into the wet ingredients at the beginning of the recipe. I like to use the "crunchy" kind, but the smooth is also good.

Coffee Carob Cake
Add 2 tbsp. Pero instant breakfast drink or instant coffee (decaffeinated recommended) mixed with 1 tbsp. hot water. Blend with wet ingredients at the beginning of the recipe.

Carob Orange Cake
Add 2 tsp. pure orange extract instead of vanilla extract.

CREAM CAKES

If you want to impress anyone (or yourself), take the few extra moments necessary to assemble these creamy delights. All of these cakes are best eaten the same day they are made because you want the optimum moistness combined with the soft cream.

Coconutty Cream Cake

Because equal amounts of flour and coconut are used, you can be sure to taste the great coconut flavor. Contains potassium and phosphorus.

1/2 c. butter (one cube)
   room temp.
1 c. honey
2 eggs
2 c. granulated unsweetened
   coconut

2 c. whole-wheat pastry flour
1 tsp. baking powder
1 tsp. baking soda
1/2 tsp. sea salt
3/4 c. whole milk
1/2 c. buttermilk

Preheat oven to 350°

Blend butter and honey until smooth and creamy. Beat in eggs, then coconut. In a separate bowl, sift together flour, baking powder, baking soda, and salt. Set aside. In a measuring cup (2-cup capacity), measure and mix milk and buttermilk. Alternately add flour mixture and milks to wet ingredients. Scrape bowl occasionally so that all ingredients are evenly mixed. Pour batter into two round 8" cake tins that are buttered and floured. Bake 25-30 minutes or until lightly browned on top and a toothpick inserted in center of cake comes out clean. Frost with Fresh Whipped-Cream Frosting.

Fresh Whipped-Cream Frosting
2 c. whipping cream
2 tbsp. honey
1 tsp. pure vanilla extract

Whip cream at high speed with an electric mixer, or vigorously by hand, using a wire whisk, until cream starts to thicken. Add honey and vanilla and continue to whip until cream is thick and stiff. Be sure cake is completely cooled since slightest warmth from cake will melt whipped cream. Frost cake and store covered in a refrigerator.

Pumpkin Spice Cream Cake

This cake is a refreshing change from pumpkin pie and is far too good to serve just around the holidays. Pumpkin is very high in vitamin A, plus smaller amounts of potassium, thiamin, riboflavin, and vitamin C.

3/4 c. safflower oil	2 c. whole-wheat pastry flour
3/4 c. honey	1 1/2 tsp. baking soda
2 eggs	2 tsp. cinnamon
2 tsp. pure vanilla extract	1 1/2 tsp. ginger
1 c. pureed pumpkin (fresh cooked or from a can)	3/4 tsp. cloves
	1/2 tsp. sea salt

Preheat oven to 350°

Blend oil, honey, eggs, and vanilla until oil and honey do not separate. Mix in pumpkin. In a separate bowl, sift together flour, baking soda, spices, and salt. Gradually add to wet ingredients, mixing well after each addition. Blend until batter is smooth and creamy. Pour batter into two round 8" cake tins that are buttered and floured. Bake 25-30 minutes or until slightly firm on top and a toothpick inserted in center of cake comes out clean. After cake has completely cooled, cut each layer in half horizontally, using a serrated knife. Spread a small amount of Whipped Cream Frosting on one layer and down the sides. Place another layer over it and spread whipped cream over top and sides of that layer. Continue process until cake is complete. Keep cake covered and stored in a refrigerator.

Honey Spice Cream Cake

The wonderful liquid sweetness of honey gives you not only a delicious taste, but also many nutrients. They are potassium, phosphorus, calcium, iron, and vitamin B-6 to name just a few.

1/2 c. butter (one cube) room temp.	1 tsp. baking powder
1 c. honey	2 tsp. cinnamon
2 eggs	1 tsp. nutmeg
1 tsp. pure vanilla extract	1/2 tsp. cloves
2 c. whole-wheat pastry flour	1/4 tsp. sea salt
1 tsp. baking soda	1/2 c. whole milk
	1/2 c. buttermilk

Preheat oven to 350°

Blend butter and honey till smooth. Add eggs and vanilla and beat until light and fluffy. Set aside. In a separate bowl sift together flour, baking soda, baking powder, spices, and salt. Combine milk and buttermilk and, alternating with flour mixture, add to wet ingredients, ending with flour. Beat until smooth and creamy. Pour batter into two round 8" cake tins that are buttered and floured. Bake 25-30 minutes or until slightly firm and browned on top and a toothpick inserted in center of cake comes out clean. Let cake cool completely and frost with Fresh Whipped-Cream Frosting.

Fresh Whipped-Cream Frosting
  2 c. whipping cream
  2 tbsp. honey
  1 tsp. pure vanilla extract

Whip cream at high speed with an electric mixer, or vigorously by hand, using a wire whisk, until cream starts to thicken. Add honey and vanilla and continue to whip until cream is thick and stiff. Be sure cake is completely cooled since slightest warmth from cake will melt whipped cream. Frost cake and store covered in a refrigerator.

Fresh Strawberry and Lemon Cream Cake

A different kind of strawberry shortcake

This cake was very popular at the restaurant during the hot summer months—but it tastes great year around. Fresh sliced strawberries are nestled between four moist layers of tart lemon cake. Contains vitamins A and C, plus potassium.

1/2 c. butter (one cube) room temp.	1 1/2 tsp. baking soda
1 c. honey	1/4 tsp. sea salt
3 eggs	1/2 c. whole milk
1 tbsp. pure lemon extract	1/2 c. buttermilk
2 1/2 c. unbleached white flour	

Preheat oven to 350°

Blend butter and honey until smooth and creamy. Add eggs and lemon extract and continue beating until well blended. In a separate bowl sift together flour, baking soda, and salt. Combine milk and buttermilk and, alternating with flour, add to wet ingredients, beating until batter is smooth after each addition. Pour batter into two round 8" cake tins that are buttered and floured. Bake 25-30 minutes or until top is lightly browned and a toothpick inserted in center of cake comes out clean.

Fresh Strawberry Filling
1 pint basket fresh strawberries *or*
    1 12-oz. package unsweetened fresh-frozen strawberries
1 tbsp. pure vanilla extract

Remove stems from all but three strawberries and thinly slice. Place strawberries in a bowl and toss with vanilla extract. Set aside. Prepare Fresh Whipped-Cream Frosting (see page 26). After cake has cooled completely, cut each layer in half horizontally, using a serrated knife. Spread a thin layer of whipped-cream frosting on bottom layer of cake. Place only enough strawberry slices on top of frosting to cover cake. Place next layer on top and proceed with the same method. After second layer is in place, frost sides of cake. Repeat process with remaining two layers. Decorate top of cake with three uncut strawberries. Cover cake and store in a refrigerator.

Cappuccino Cream Cake

This is the queen of the cream cakes.

Contains calcium, phosphorus, potassium, protein, and some iron.

1 c. safflower oil
1 c. buttermilk
1 c. honey
2 eggs
1 tsp. pure orange extract
1 tbsp. Pero or instant coffee
    (decaffeinated recommended)
1 tbsp. very hot water
2 c. whole-wheat pastry flour

1 1/2 tsp. cinnamon
1 tsp. nutmeg
1/2 tsp. cloves
1/2 tsp. sea salt
1 tsp. baking soda
1 tsp. baking powder
1/3 c. unsweetened, roasted
carob powder

Preheat oven to 350°

Blend oil, buttermilk, honey, and eggs until oil and honey do not separate. Combine Pero (or coffee) with hot water and add to other ingredients together with orange extract. In a separate bowl, sift together flour, spices, salt, baking soda, baking powder, and carob powder. Add dry ingredients to wet and blend until creamy. Pour batter into two round 8" cake tins that are buttered and floured. Bake 30-35 minutes or until a toothpick inserted in center of cake comes out clean. Prepare Coffee Cream Frosting. After cake has cooled, cut each layer in half horizontally, using a serrated knife. Spread frosting evenly over first layer. Place next layer on top and frost top and sides. Repeat process with next two layers. Cover cake and store in a refrigerator.

Coffee Cream Frosting
2 1/2 c. whipping cream
3 tbsp. honey
1 tbsp. Pero or instant coffee (decaffeinated recommended)
1 tbsp. very hot water
1 tsp. pure orange extract
1/2 tsp. cinnamon
1/4 tsp. nutmeg
1/4 tsp. cloves

Combine Pero (or coffee) with hot water, set aside to cool. Whip cream at high speed with electric mixer, or vigorously by hand using a wire whisk, until cream starts to thicken. Add honey and extract, whip until blended. Add cooled Pero (or coffee), then spices, continue whipping until cream is thick and stiff.

White-Ginger Cream Cake

Having an Oriental dinner? This cake would make a perfect end to your meal. Contains calcium, protein, and some vitamin A.

1/2 c. butter (one cube) room temp.	3 tsp. powdered ginger
1 c. honey	1 tsp. baking powder
1 tsp. pure vanilla extract	1 tsp. baking soda
2 eggs	1/4 tsp. sea salt
2 c. whole-wheat pastry flour	1/4 c. + 1 tbsp. buttermilk
	1/2 c. milk

Preheat oven to 350°

Blend butter and honey until smooth and creamy. Add eggs and vanilla, mix until well blended. In a separate bowl sift together flour, ginger, and baking soda. Blend into wet ingredients. Batter will be thick. Combine buttermilk and milk and slowly add to batter, beating well after each addition. Batter will still be slightly thick. Spread batter evenly into two round 8" cake tins that are buttered and floured. Bake 25-30 minutes or until top of cake is lightly browned and a toothpick inserted in center of cake comes out clean. After cake has completely cooled, cut each layer in half horizontally, using a serrated knife. Spread whipped cream evenly on top of first layer. Place another layer of cake on top of first and frost. Continue process with other layers. Frost top and sides with remaining whipped cream. Cake is best eaten the day it is made. Keep any remaining cake covered in a refrigerator.

Orange Whipped-Cream Frosting
    2 c. whipping cream
    2 tsp. pure orange extract
    2 tbsp. honey

Whip cream at high speed with an electric mixer, or vigorously by hand using a wire whisk, until cream starts to thicken. Add extract and honey and continue whipping until cream is thick and stiff.

Piña Colada Cream Cake

Taste the tropics in this light, cool dessert! Great to have during those hot summer months. Contains some niacin, iron, and riboflavin, with larger amounts of vitamin A and potassium.

1/2 c. butter (one cube)
    room temp.
1 c. fructose
2 eggs
2 c. unsweetened granulated
    coconut
2 c. unbleached white flour
1 tsp. baking powder
1 tsp. baking soda

1/2 tsp. sea salt
3/4 c. pineapple juice or
    pineapple-coconut juice
1/2 c. milk
1 1/2 tsp. pure rum extract
    (available at health-food
    stores, contains no sugar
    or alcohol)

Preheat oven to 350°

Blend butter and fructose until smooth and creamy. Beat in eggs and coconut. In separate bowl sift together flour, baking powder, baking soda, and salt. Mix together juice, milk, and extract and add to wet ingredients, beating until well blended. Blend in dry ingredients a little at a time and beat together until creamy. Pour batter into two round 8" cake tins that are buttered and floured. Bake 25-30 minutes or until lightly browned on top and a toothpick inserted in center of cake comes out clean. After cake has cooled completely, cut each layer in half horizontally, using a serrated knife. Spread Pineapple Cream Frosting on first layer, then about 1/4 cup of pineapple. Continue process to top of cake. *Do not* add pineapple to top of cake. Frost top with whipped cream only. Cake is best eaten the day it is made. Keep any remaining cake covered in a refrigerator.

Pineapple Cream Frosting
    2 1/2 c. heavy cream
    3 tbsp. honey
    1/2 tsp. pure rum extract (nonalcoholic)
    3/4 c. crushed pineapple (fresh, or unsweetened from the can)

Whip cream at high speed with an electric mixer, or vigorously by hand using a wire whisk, until cream starts to thicken. Add honey and extract and continue whipping until cream is thick and stiff.

BUNDT CAKES

Bundt cakes make a nice addition to any break-fast or brunch. Their texture is somewhat between cake and bread. They are a little sweeter than bread, but not as sweet as cake.

Carob-Chip Coconut Bundt Cake

A candy bar in a cake! Contains potassium, phosphorus, and some protein.

1/2 c. butter (one cube)
room temp.
1/2 c. date sugar
1/2 c. honey
2 eggs
2 tbsp. fresh lemon juice
1 c. whole milk
1/4 c. buttermilk

2 c. whole-wheat pastry flour
1 1/2 tsp. baking soda
1/4 tsp. sea salt
1/2 c. grated unsweetened
coconut
1 c. date-sweetened carob
chips

Preheat oven to 350°

Blend butter, date sugar, and honey. Beat in eggs. Add lemon juice, milk, and buttermilk, and blend well. In a separate bowl sift flour, baking soda, and salt. Gradually add dry ingredients to wet and beat until batter is smooth and creamy. Fold in coconut and carob chips last. Pour batter into a buttered and floured bundt pan. Bake 40-45 minutes or until lightly browned on top and a toothpick inserted in center of cake comes out clean. Store in a covered container.

Poppy-Seed Bundt Cake

Makes an excellent brunch or breakfast cake. Not too sweet, and spiced with a hint of cinnamon. Vitamin A, calcium, protein, and fiber.

3/4 c. butter (1 1/2 cubes) room temp.
1/2 c. fructose
1/2 c. date sugar
1 tbsp. Pero or instant coffee (decaffeinated recommended)
1 tbsp. very hot water
1 tbsp. poppy seeds

2 eggs
2 1/2 c. whole-wheat pastry flour
1 1/2 tsp. baking soda
2 tsp. cinnamon
1/2 tsp. sea salt
1 tsp. pure vanilla extract
1 1/4 c. whole milk

Preheat oven to 350°

Combine Pero (or coffee), hot water, and poppy seeds. Blend butter, fructose, date sugar, and Pero (or coffee). Beat in eggs. Sift together flour, baking soda, cinnamon, and salt in a separate bowl and set aside. In a third container blend milk and vanilla. Alternating milk and dry ingredients, gradually add to wet ingredients, mixing well after each addition until batter is well blended and creamy. Pour batter into buttered and floured bundt pan. Bake 35-40 minutes or until a toothpick inserted in center of cake comes out clean. Store in a covered container.

3—P.C.

Anise Bundt Cake

Unique and delicious. Compliments hot drinks, fresh fruit, and cheeses. Contains vitamin A and calcium.

1/2 c. butter (one cube)
   room temp.
3/4 c. honey
2 eggs
2 tsp. pure anise extract

2 c. whole-wheat pastry flour
1 1/2 tsp. baking soda
1/2 tsp. sea salt
1/2 c. whole milk
1/2 c. heavy cream

Preheat oven to 350°

Blend together butter and honey until smooth. Beat in eggs and extract. Sift in flour, baking soda, and salt. Mix together milk and cream slowly, blending well after each addition. Continue to blend batter until smooth and creamy. Pour batter into a buttered and floured bundt pan. Bake 30-35 minutes or until lightly browned on top and a toothpick inserted in center of cake comes out clean. Store covered in a cool place.

Coffee Swirl Bundt Cake

What is a brunch without coffee cake? Light and tasty with just enough pecans for a mild flavor. Potassium, thiamin, iron, and riboflavin.

Preheat oven to 375°

Step 1: The Batter

1/2 c. butter (one cube) room temp.	2 tsp. cinnamon
3/4 c. honey	1 tsp. baking powder
2 eggs	1 tsp. baking soda
1 tsp. pure vanilla extract	1/2 tsp. sea salt
2 c. whole-wheat pastry flour	3/4 c. buttermilk

Blend butter and honey until smooth and creamy. Beat in eggs and vanilla. Combine dry ingredients and add gradually to wet ingredients, alternating with buttermilk. Blend until batter is thick and creamy.

Step 2: The Coffee Swirl
1 tbsp. Pero or instant coffee (decaffeinated recommended)
1 tbsp. very hot water

Dissolve Pero (or coffee) in hot water and set it aside to cool to room temperature (approx. 3 minutes). Add to batter and fold in just slightly, *not* thoroughly. Pour half of batter into a buttered and floured bundt pan.

Step 3: The Filling
1/4 c. grated unsweetened coconut
1/2 c. finely chopped pecans
1 tbsp. fructose
1/2 tsp. cinnamon
1/4 tsp. nutmeg

Blend coconut, pecans, fructose, and spices. Sprinkle on top of batter in pan. Spread remaining batter over filling mixture. Bake 30-35 minutes or until lightly browned on top and a toothpick inserted in center of cake comes out clean. Serve warm. Store any remaining cake in a covered container.

Peanut-Butter-and-Jelly Bundt Cake

For the kid in all of us! Peanut butter contains potassium, calcium, and protein.

1/2 c. butter (one cube) room temp.
3/4 c. honey
2 eggs
3 tbsp. crunchy peanut butter
2 tsp. pure vanilla extract
1 tsp. baking powder
1 tsp. baking soda

1 c. whole milk
1 tsp. sea salt (if peanut butter is *un*salted) *or*
1/2 tsp. sea salt (if peanut butter is salted)
2 c. whole-wheat pastry flour
1/2 c. honey- or fruit-juice sweetened jelly

Preheat oven to 350°

Blend butter, honey, and peanut butter. Add eggs and vanilla, and blend until batter is light and fluffy. In a separate bowl sift flour, baking powder, baking soda, and salt. Alternating dry ingredients and milk, gradually add to wet ingredients, blending well after each addition. Batter will be thick and fluffy. Spread into a buttered and floured bundt pan. Bake 40-45 minutes or until lightly browned on top and a toothpick inserted in center of cake comes out clean. (Be sure to test this cake carefully because it can look done on the outside and still not be fully baked on the inside.) After cake has cooled, spread your favorite jelly on top, allowing some jelly to drip down sides. Store cake at room temperature in a covered container.

Maple Walnut Bundt Cake

Maple syrup and walnuts are always a delicious combination. This cake is extra moist and has a mild maple flavor. Maple syrup provides iron, calcium, and potassium.

1/2 c. butter (one cube) room temp.	1/2 c. buttermilk
1 1/4 c. pure maple syrup	2 c. whole-wheat pastry flour
2 eggs	1 tsp. baking powder
1/2 tsp. pure orange extract	1 tsp. baking soda
	1/2 tsp. sea salt

Preheat oven to 350°

Blend butter and maple syrup. Beat in eggs. Add orange extract and buttermilk. Sift together flour, baking powder, baking soda, and salt and add to wet ingredients a little at a time, blending well after each addition. (There may be a few lumps from the butter.) Pour batter into a buttered and floured bundt pan. Bake 35-40 minutes or until a toothpick inserted in center of cake comes out clean. Remove cake from pan while it is still warm, *not hot*. Add topping.

Topping
1/2 c. finely chopped walnuts
1 tbsp. butter
1 tbsp. pure maple syrup
1 tsp. pure orange extract

Melt butter over a low flame. Do *not* brown. Add walnuts and stir until walnuts are all coated with butter. Remove from heat, add maple syrup and extract, stirring until well blended. Spread on top of cake. Store cake at room temperature in a covered container.

Healthful and Wholesome Dyes You Can Make Yourself

Here are a few easy ways to make your own dyes. Some colors take a little more time than others, but the results are worth it. Be cautious when adding liquid dyes to your frosting. Add them in small amounts so you can watch the consistency. Half a teaspoonful at a time is a good way to start. Runny frosting is difficult to spread on a cake or to squeeze through a pastry tube for decorating.

Brown—Use unsweetened, roasted carob powder
Blend into frosting a teaspoonful at a time until you achieve the shade of brown you want. Add fructose or honey to your taste.

Green—Use chlorophyll (liquid form)
Chlorophyll is the green matter that is extracted from leaves and plants. It contains various minerals and makes a great mouthwash when mixed with water. You will probably need at least a teaspoonful of chlorophyll to obtain a light green color, more for darker. When tightly capped, chlorophyll will last for months.

Orange—Use carrot juice
Bring half a cup of *day old* carrot juice to a boil. Stir occasionally so liquid does not burn. As juice foams and separates from liquid, scrape off foam and place in a small bowl to cool; then stir a teaspoonful at a time into frosting. Carrot sediment does not keep long, so is best made fresh as needed.

Pink—Use fresh beet juice
Place one medium-size beet in a blender and grind until well shredded. Pour juice into a cup and place shredded beet on a cheesecloth. Squeeze out remaining juice. Beet juice will not keep long, so is best made fresh as needed.

Yellow—Use tumeric
Tumeric is a spice found in many Indian dishes. Though it has a distinctive flavor, it will not interfere with the flavor of the frosting. Please note that the longer tumeric is in the frosting, the darker it will get on its own, so be conservative. Wait a few minutes before adding more.

PIES

The following pies burst with freshness and flavor, and are as "easy as pie" to make.

Hints for Making A Perfect Pie Crust

Many people feel intimidated about making pies. Don't be! A cooking teacher of mine once told the class that pie making has lots of "therapeutic" benefits: What other dessert can you actually feel, poke, pinch, and mold? The following directions will turn your doughmaking into a pleasant experience:

1. Before mixing your dough, be sure the butter or margarine is cold and cut into pieces, a little bigger than a pea. I use a grater for this. As the butter mixes with the flour it coats the particles of flour and prevents the formation of gluten. This helps to keep the crust tender. The rest of the butter melts when the crust is baked, forming tiny pockets in the dough that fill up with steam. This creates a flaky pie crust. Although butter works best to develop this process, margarine is more than satisfactory. One of the recipes on the next page is for a butter crust, the other for a margarine crust.

2. Coat your counter or cutting board and your rolling pin with a small amount of flour (enough to leave a thin film) and brush aside any excess.

3. Mold a flat circle of dough in your hands. Do not knead it. Place the dough in the center of the floured cutting board or counter.

4. Roll the dough out in one direction only. Do not roll the rolling pin back and forth. You may need to pick up the dough and turn it slightly to make this step easier for you.

5. Turn the dough over and roll it out about an inch larger than the required size. You may need to cover your cutting board (or counter) and rolling pin with flour again.

6. Carefully lift the dough from the surface and place it in the pie plate. Try not to stretch the dough. Ease it gently into the pie plate.

7. Form the dough to the shape of the pie plate, leaving about a half inch overhang. Turn this under the lip of the pie plate.

8. After the pie ingredients are added, if an upper crust is needed, center and place the upper crust on top of the ingredients and poke several tiny holes through the top of the crust. A pie crust without holes may shrink.

9. To make a finished edge, place one thumb on the outer edge of the pie plate. With your other thumb and index finger carefully yet firmly press the dough

up and around both sides of your stationary thumb. Continue this process around the edge of the pie. When making a pie which requires both a top and bottom crust, make sure the crusts meet all around, and then tuck under a small amount of dough in three or four places and press firmly.

The Basic Pie Crust

The following two Basic Pie Crust recipes are moist to roll out and flaky when baked. Both can be made by using a pastry blender or two forks. See the previous section for hints on making a perfect pie crust.

Basic Pie Crust 1
    2 c. whole-wheat pastry flour
    3/4 tsp. sea salt
    1/2 c. cold butter (one cube) cut into small pieces
    1/4 c. (or a little more) cold water

Basic Pie Crust 2
    1 c. whole-wheat pastry flour
    1 c. unbleached white flour
    1/2 tsp. sea salt
    1/2 c. cold natural margarine (one cube) cut into small pieces
    1/4 c. (or a little more) cold water

With a pastry blender or two forks (whichever is more comfortable for you) blend flour or flours, salt, and butter or margarine pieces until butter or margarine is evenly mixed in and flour resembles coarse meal. Add water slowly, using only enough so dough holds together and cleans sides of bowl. Dough should be moist and workable. Roll dough out on a floured cutting board. Yield: Two 9" or 10" pie crusts. (Please note that number 2 recipe may need 5-10 minutes more baking time. Since this time is estimated, take a few extra peeks into oven during final stages of baking time.)

Fresh Apple Pie

This pie is packed full of fresh, tart apples and complimented with raisins and walnuts. Apples are a good source of vitamins A and C plus iron and phosphorus.

2 unbaked 9" or 10" pie crusts
5-6 pippin apples, cored but unpeeled, and sliced into thin wedges
1/3 c. unsweetened apple juice
1/4 c. fresh squeezed lemon juice

1/4 c. + 1 tbsp. honey
1/4 c. melted butter (1/2 cube)
1 tsp. cinnamon
3 tbsp. arrowroot
1/4 c. chopped walnuts
1/4 c. unsulfured raisins

Preheat oven to 375°

Place a crust on bottom and sides of a 9" or 10" pie plate. Cut excess dough from edge of plate. In a bowl, mix together apples, apple juice, and lemon juice. Cover bottom of pie plate with apples, and sprinkle one tablespoonful of arrowroot on top. Add half of remaining apples and sprinkle another tablespoonful of arrowroot on top. Add cinnamon, nuts, and raisins, spacing evenly between apples. Add remaining apples and juice, and pour melted butter mixed with honey evenly over top. Sprinkle last tablespoonful of arrowroot over all ingredients and cover pie with remaining crust. Finish edge around pie (see "Hints For Making a Perfect Pie Crust" on page 40) and poke several tiny holes in top with a fork. Bake 55-60 minutes or until top and sides of pie are lightly browned. Cool pie completely before covering, and store in a refrigerator. May be served warm or cold.

Plump and Juicy Peach Pie

Peach pie has always been a favorite of mine. Even after peaches are baked, they still burst with juice and flavor. Vitamins A, C, and potassium are just a few of the nutrients found in this pie.

2 unbaked 9" or 10" pie
   crusts
5-6 medium-size ripe peaches,
   unpeeled, pitted, and sliced
   into medium-size wedges

1/4 c. warm water (not hot)
1/4 c. honey
2 tbsp. arrowroot

Preheat oven to 375°

Place a crust on bottom and sides of a 9" or 10" pie plate. Cut excess dough from edge of plate. Arrange half of the peaches evenly on bottom of plate. Sprinkle one tablespoonful of arrowroot over peaches and arrange remaining peaches on top. Sprinkle second tablespoonful of arrowroot over peaches. Combine honey and warm water, stirring until honey is dissolved. Pour sweetened water over peaches and cover pie with second crust. Finish edge around pie (see "Hints for Making a Perfect Pie Crust," page 40) and poke several tiny holes in top crust with a fork. Bake 55-60 minutes or until top and sides of crust are lightly browned. Cool pie completely before covering, and store in a refrigerator. May be served warm or cold.

Fresh Banana Cream Pie

Fresh bananas mixed with banana cream make this pie extra smooth, yet rich in banana taste. Bananas are filled with potassium and vitamins A and C, and the cream gives you extra protein.

Preheat oven to 375°

Step 1: The Banana Cream

1 unbaked 9"or 10" pie crust	2 eggs
3 medium-size ripe, but firm bananas	2 tbsp. honey
	2/3 c. whole milk

Place crust in a 9" or 10" pie plate. Peel and cut bananas into small pieces and place in a mixing bowl along with eggs and honey. Blend until bananas are mashed up. Add milk and continue blending until mixture is fairly smooth (do not worry about a few lumps). Pour mixture into prepared pie plate and bake 30-35 minutes, or until sides of crust are lightly browned and banana cream is firm. Cool to room temperature.

Step 2: The Middle

2 medium-size firm, ripe bananas

Cut bananas into thin, round slices and place evenly on top of baked pie.

Step 3: The Topping

1 c. heavy cream
1 tbsp. honey

Whip cream at high speed with an electric mixer, or vigorously by hand using a wire whisk, until it starts to thicken. Add honey and continue whipping until cream is thick and stiff. Spread fresh whipped cream evenly on top of pie and sliced bananas. Serve cold and keep refrigerated.

Quick and Easy Custard Pear Pie

This pie has somewhat of a custardlike quality. Pears contain potassium.

1 unbaked 9" or 10" pie crust
2 16-oz. cans of pear halves
    packed in unsweetened juice
3/4 c. juice from pears

2 tbsp. honey
1 tbsp. fresh lemon juice
2 eggs

Preheat oven to 375°

Place crust in 9" or 10" pie plate. Arrange pears decoratively on crust. Whip juice, honey, lemon juice, and eggs until well blended and eggs are evenly mixed in. Pour liquid over top of pears and bake 35-40 minutes or until edges of crust are brown and liquid is set. Serve warm or cold.

Cold Fresh-Strawberry Pie

When used with Basic Pie Crust 2, this is a delicious nondairy dessert for those watching their dairy intake. Strawberries are rich in vitamins C and A, plus potassium.

Preheat oven to 375°

Step 1: The Crust
>   **1 unbaked 9" or 10" pie crust**
>   **2 cups dry beans or rice**

Place crust in a 9" or 10" pie plate. Press a piece of foil, shiny side down, over crust and place beans or rice on top (this holds dough in place and minimizes shrinking). Bake 15-20 minutes. Remove foil, and beans or rice, and continue baking another 10 minutes. Allow to cool.

Step 2: The Filling
>   **2 pint baskets fresh strawberries** **4 tbsp. honey**
>   **(stems removed)** **4 tbsp. agar**
>   **1 c. unsweetened apple juice** **1 c. fresh whipped cream**
>   **or apple-strawberry juice** **(optional for garnish)**

Place cut sides of strawberries on top of baked and cooled crust. Cook juice, honey, and agar over a medium flame, stirring occasionally until liquid comes to a boil. Reduce heat and simmer 2 minutes. Pour hot liquid over strawberries in pie plate and refrigerate until liquid is set (about 3 hours). Serve cold, with or without whipped cream. Cover pie and store in a refrigerator.

Southern Bean Pie

This pie is similar in taste to pumpkin pie, but has a southern twist. High in potassium, calcium, phosphorus, and protein.

1 unbaked 9" or 10" pie crust
2 c. cooked, drained, mashed
   pinto beans*
1/2 c. honey
1/4 c. butter (1/2 cube)
   room temp.
3 eggs

1 tsp. pure vanilla extract
2 tsp. cinnamon
1 tsp. nutmeg
1/2 tsp. cloves
1/4 tsp. sea salt
1 c. fresh whipped cream
   (optional for topping)

Preheat oven to 375°

Place crust in a 9" or 10" pie plate. Blend beans, honey, and butter until smooth and creamy. Add eggs and vanilla and continue beating until well blended. Add spices and salt and blend evenly. Pour into crust and bake 45-50 minutes or until crust is light brown and liquid is set. Serve warm or cold, with or without fresh whipped cream. Pie should be stored in a refrigerator.

*2 16-oz. cans of pinto beans will work, but freshly cooked beans are better.

Honey Custard Pie

Or "High Protein Pie" because of its large amounts of protein, plus vitamins A and B-6, calcium, and potassium. A light and creamy dessert.

1 unbaked 9" or 10" pie crust	1/2 c. honey
2 c. whole milk	1/2 tsp. pure vanilla extract
4 extra large eggs	1/2 tsp. cinnamon

Preheat oven to 350°

Whip milk, eggs, honey, and vanilla until well blended and eggs are evenly mixed in. Liquid should be light and opaque. Pour liquid into prepared pie crust and bake 50-55 minutes or until set so that a knife, when inserted in center of pie, comes out clean. Sprinkle top with cinnamon while still hot. Serve warm or cold.

The Best Cheesecake*

Some people feel that whole-grain desserts can never quite compare to the "real thing." This cheesecake proves them wrong! It is rich, thick, creamy, and wonderful. The nutritional benefits of this dessert are protein, vitamins A and C, and calcium.

Preheat oven to 375°

This recipe requires an 11" springform pan (removable sides and pitted bottom, available at most cookware stores).

Step 1: The Crust
1 c. walnuts	1/4 c. butter (1/2 cube)
1 c. almonds	1 c. whole carob cookies

Chop walnuts, almonds, and cookies in small amounts in a blender until finely ground. (Turning blender on and off helps mixture to move around.) Place mixture in a bowl. Melt butter over a low flame (avoid browning), pour over nut mixture, and blend. Press into bottom (not sides) of springform pan, especially around edges to prevent leakage after batter is added.

Step 2: The Filling
2 1/2 c. cream cheese (room temp.)	5 eggs
1 c. cottage cheese (small curd)	1 c. honey
1 c. sour cream	1 tbsp. pure vanilla extract

Blend cream cheese, cottage cheese, and sour cream until creamy (there will be some lumps in batter from cottage cheese). Add eggs, honey, and vanilla. Beat until well blended, making sure honey does not sink to bottom. In small amounts, run batter through a blender until completely smooth and creamy. Pour batter into prepared springform pan, filling 2/3, leaving room for cheesecake to rise. Place cheesecake on a cookie sheet and bake 60-65 minutes or until lightly browned on top and center is set. Cheesecake may crack.

Step 3: The Topping
1 1/2 c. heavy cream	1/4 c. honey
1 tsp. pure vanilla extract	

Whip cream at high speed with an electric mixer, or vigorously by hand using a wire whisk, until it starts to thicken. Add honey and vanilla and continue beating until thick and stiff. Spread evenly over cooled cheesecake. Cover and store in a refrigerator.

*See Cheesecake Variations on the next page.

4—P.C.

Cheesecake Variations

You may or may not use step 3 with these variations. I think it is best with the whipped cream added.

Fresh Fruit Cheesecake
1 c. fresh fruit (strawberries, blueberries, raspberries, etc.)

Cut fruit into small pieces (blueberries and raspberries are fine as they are), and fold gently into batter *after* it has been poured into springform pan. Allow room for fruit by using less batter. Fresh fruit will make a more moist cheesecake. Use canned or very juicy fruits (such as peaches or pineapple) for topping *only,* otherwise batter will not set.

Banana Cheesecake
1 very ripe medium-size banana
1/2 tsp. nutmeg

Blend in banana when preparing batter in a blender. Banana makes cheesecake more firm. Riper bananas make richer flavor. Sprinkle top with nutmeg.

Pure Maple Walnut Cheesecake
1 1/4 c. pure maple syrup
1 c. chopped walnuts

Use maple syrup in place of honey and fold in walnuts after batter has been poured into springform pan. Maple Walnut Cheesecake is delicate, moist, and absolutely delicious.

Carob Mint Cheesecake
3 tbsp. unsweetened, roasted carob powder
1 1/2 tsp. pure spearmint or peppermint extract

Add carob powder and extract along with eggs and honey, omitting vanilla extract.

Rum Raisin Cheesecake
1 1/2 tsp. pure rum extract (nonalcoholic and sugarless)
1 c. unsulfured raisins

Omit vanilla extract and add rum extract. Fold in raisins after batter has been poured into springform pan.

Carob-Chip Cheesecake
1 c. date-sweetened carob chips

Fold in carob chips after batter has been poured into springform pan.

Cheesy Cheesecake

A true cheese cheesecake. Smooth and slightly firm. Provides linoleic acid, vitamin A, calcium, and lots of protein.

Preheat oven to 350°

This recipe requires a 10" springform pan (removable sides and pitted bottom, available at most cookware stores).

Step 1: The Crust
1 1/2 c. finely crushed (in a blender is OK) honey-sweetened graham crackers

1 tbsp. fructose
1 tsp. cinnamon
3 tbsp. melted butter

Mix graham crackers, fructose, and cinnamon. Add melted butter and blend until moistened. Press firmly into bottom (not sides) of springform pan, especially around edges to prevent leakage after batter is added.

Step 2: The Filling
1 15-oz. container of ricotta cheese
1 8-oz. package cream cheese (room temp.)
1 c. sour cream

1 c. honey
4 eggs
2 tsp. pure vanilla extract
1 tbsp. fresh lemon juice

Blend ricotta cheese and cream cheese until smooth. Add sour cream and honey, beat until well blended. Add eggs one at a time, beating well each time. Mix in vanilla and lemon juice. Pour batter into springform pan and bake 50-60 minutes or until lightly browned on top and center is set. Allow to cool completely before serving. Keep cheesecake covered and store in a refrigerator.

Blueberry-Bottom Yogurt Pie

This pie was extremely popular at the restaurant and in my bakery. It is extra smooth and creamy, with a surprise at the bottom that will keep you coming back for more. Yogurt has lots of vitamins A, C, B-1, B-6, and B-12, plus calcium and potassium.

Preheat oven to 375°

This recipe requires a 10" springform pan (removable sides and pitted bottom, available at most cookware stores).

Step 1: The Crust

1 c. walnuts	1 c. carob cookies
1 c. almonds	1/4 c. butter (1/2 cube)

Chop walnuts, almonds, and cookies in a blender half a cup at a time until finely ground. Place mixture in a bowl. Melt butter over a low flame (avoid browning), pour over mixture, and blend. Press into bottom, not sides, of springform pan, especially around edges to prevent leakage after batter is poured in.

Step 2: The Blueberry Bottom

1 10-oz. jar honey- or fruit juice-sweetened blueberry preserves

Spread preserves evenly on top of prepared crust. Set aside.

Step 3: The Filling

1 c. cottage cheese (small curd)	4 eggs
2 c. plain yogurt	1/2 c. fructose
1 1/2 c. cream cheese (room temp.)	

Blend cottage cheese, yogurt, and cream cheese until creamy (there will be some small lumps from cottage cheese). Beat in eggs one at a time until evenly blended. Stir in fructose. Run batter through a blender until completely smooth. Pour batter over crust. Place springform pan on top of a cookie sheet and bake 1 hour and 15 minutes or until lightly browned around edges and center is set. Store in refrigerator *after* pie has cooled to room temperature. Pie is best served cold directly from refrigerator. Keep pie covered to retain creamy, moist texture.

No-bake Yogurt Pie

This pie is one of Mike's* favorites. I still bake it for his birthday. It is light, creamy, smooth, and perfect to serve for brunch or at a dinner party. Contains iron, protein, calcium, vitamins A, C, B-1, B-6, and B-12.

Step 1: The Crust

1 c. rolled oats
3/4 c. chopped and pitted
    dates

1/4 c. unsweetened
    grated coconut
3 tbsp. butter

Chop oats, dates, and coconut in a blender until finely ground. Melt butter over low flame (avoid browning), and mix into dry ingredients. Press into bottom and sides of a 9" pie plate.

Step 2: The Filling

1 1/2 c. cream cheese
    (room temp.)
1 c. honey-sweetened
    vanilla yogurt

2 tbsp. honey
2 tsp. pure vanilla extract
2 tbsp. butter (room temp.)
    Do *not* use margarine

Blend cream cheese, honey, vanilla, and butter until smooth. Add yogurt and continue blending until creamy. Pour into crust and refrigerate 8 hours or overnight, until set. Pie should be covered and stored in a refrigerator.

*See Foreward by Mike Farrell.

Carob Coconut Cream Pie

The texture of this pie is between a pudding and a custard. Contains protein and calcium.

Preheat oven to 375°

Step 1: The Crust
>1 c. carob cookie crumbs
>1/2 c. unsweetened granulated coconut
>4 tbsp. melted butter

Combine the cookie crumbs, coconut, and butter in a bowl and blend thoroughly. Press mixture firmly into a 9" pie plate. Bake 10-15 minutes or until edges turn dark brown. Allow crust to cool completely and set aside. Go to step 2 *after* crust is cooled.

Step 2: The Filling
>1 1/2 c. whipping cream
>1/4 c. honey
>4 tbsp. unsweetened, roasted
>   carob powder
>
>1/2 c. unsweetened
>   grated coconut
>3 tbsp. butter (room temp.)

Whip cream at high speed with an electric mixer, or vigorously by hand using a wire whisk, until it starts to thicken. Add honey and carob powder, continuing to whip at high speed until evenly blended. Add butter and whip until thick and stiff. Fold in coconut last. Scoop cream onto prepared crust and refrigerate 2 hours.

Step 3: The Topping (optional)
This pie is great topped with fresh fruit. Try sliced bananas, strawberries, or raspberries.

TARTS

Tarts are especially fun because you can be creative with the fruit since it isn't covered by a top crust. A tart is something like a fancy pie. It has a bottom crust that is covered with a rich, thick cream and topped with fresh fruit. On the next few pages I have drawn some of my favorite fruit and design combinations, but let the artist in you come out, and make up some of your own. Remember to consider color and taste combinations when selecting your fruit.

Basic Tart Recipe

Preheat oven to 400°

Yield: One 11" tart crust (preferably use a tart pan with a removable bottom)

Step 1: The Tart Crust

2 c. unbleached white flour
1/4 tsp. sea salt
3/4 c. cold butter cut into
    small pieces (I use a grater)

1 1/2 tsp honey
1/3 c. water
3 c. dry beans or rice
11" piece of round foil*

Making a tart crust is almost like making a pie crust. Dissolve honey in tepid water and set aside. With a pastry blender or two forks (whichever is more comfortable for you), blend flour, salt, and butter pieces until butter is evenly mixed in and flour resembles course meal. Add sweetened water slowly and only enough so that dough holds together and is moist, workable, and cleans sides of bowl. Do *not* overmix. Dough is now ready to roll out. On a lightly floured cutting board or counter, roll dough out about 2 1/2" larger than tart pan. Gently ease dough into tart pan and lightly press down and around fluted edge. Cut away excess. Lay foil on top of dough (shiny side down) and top with dry beans or rice. Bake 20 minutes. Remove from oven and carefully remove beans or rice and foil. Return the crust to the oven and bake for another 10 minutes or until slightly browned in spots. Remove and cool to room temperature.

*Place a piece of foil on top of tart pan and press down slightly to make an impression. Cut off excess with scissors.

Step 2: Creamy Custard Filling

2 1/2 c. very warm
    whole milk (not scalding)
6 egg yolks, lightly beaten
4 tbsp. honey

4 tbsp. unbleached white
    flour
3 tsp. pure vanilla extract*
3 tsp. butter

Fresh fruit: strawberries, raspberries, pears, peaches. Amount of fruit needed will depend on fruit combinations.

Warm egg yolks and honey over a medium flame. Blend, but avoid cooking too much or you will have sweet scrambled eggs. Add warmed milk, stirring slowly, frequently. Add flour a tablespoonful at a time and continue stirring until mixture becomes thick and creamy. Dissolve lumps that form when adding the flour. Remove from heat and blend in butter and extract. Pour thick cream into cooled tart crust. Top cream with selected fresh fruit. Remove metal side ring and store covered in a refrigerator.

On the next page I have drawn a few diagrams of my favorite fruit combinations and some ways to decorate your tart just to give you some ideas. Don't stop there. There are plenty of variations you can make up yourself.

*For a wonderful taste change, take advantage of the many pure extracts available to you: strawberry, cherry, and a lot more.

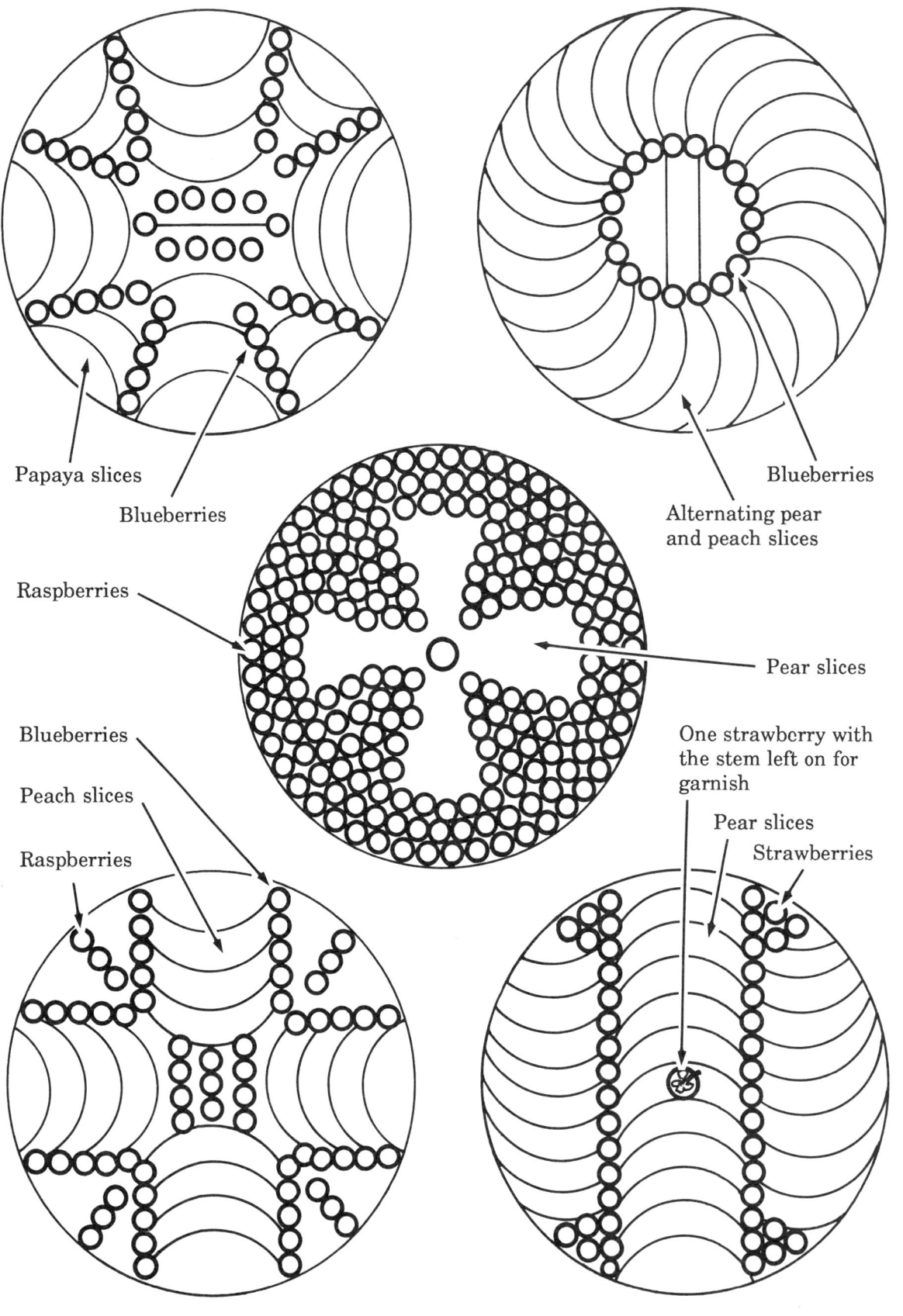

COOKIES

Here are some recipes to help fill your cookie jar. The cookies vary greatly in both taste and texture. Some are more cakelike, others snap, but all of them will melt in your mouth!

Basic Butter Cookies

Butter cookies are not only tasty and plain, but they are also versatile. Try some of the variations below. One of the reasons I like them so much is that you can take advantage of their "plainness": add a variety of ingredients, and they still taste great. Butter gives you vitamin A and potassium, calcium, and phosphorus.

1 c. butter (two cubes) room temp.	2 c. whole-wheat pastry flour
3/4 c. fructose	1/2 tsp. sea salt
1 tsp. pure vanilla extract	1/2 tsp. baking soda
1 egg	1 tsp. nutmeg

Preheat oven to 375°

Blend butter and fructose until creamy. Add egg and vanilla, beating until light and fluffy. Combine dry ingredients and add to wet ingredients. Mix batter until smooth and creamy. Using a teaspoon, drop dough onto ungreased cookie sheet and bake 8-10 minutes, or until lightly browned on top. Makes approximately 3 dozen cookies.

Variations

Here are some of my favorite variations, but have fun adding some of your own. Mix in one or more of the following with the dry ingredients.

1 tbsp. poppy seeds	1 c. date-sweetened carob chips
1 c. chopped nuts	1 1/2 tsp. cinnamon
1 c. unsulfured raisins	1 c. unsulphured dried fruit
1 c. unsweetened grated coconut	

Lemon Coconut Cookies

This cookie is mild and slightly tart. I like them with a hot drink. Contains vitamins A, C, and potassium.

3/4 c. butter (1 1/2 cube)
    room temp.
1 c. fructose
1 egg
1 tsp. pure lemon extract
1 tsp. freshly grated
    lemon rind

1 c. unsweetened
    grated coconut
2 c. unbleached white flour
1/2 tsp. cream of tartar
3/4 tsp. baking soda
1/2 tsp. sea salt

Preheat oven to 375°

Blend together butter and fructose until creamy. Add egg, lemon extract, and lemon rind, and beat until light and fluffy. Add cream of tartar and continue beating a minute more. Combine flour, coconut, baking soda, and salt in a separate bowl, making sure that coconut is evenly mixed in. Add dry ingredients to wet and blend until creamy. Dough will be slightly thick. Using a teaspoon, drop dough onto ungreased cookie sheet and bake 6-8 minutes. Cookies will brown quickly, so watch them more carefully than most other cookies. Cookies are done when lightly browned on top and around edges. Makes approximately 2 1/2 dozen cookies.

Oatmeal Almond Cookies

A tasty change from the popular oatmeal walnut cookies. Lots of natural fiber with protein, potassium, phosphorus, and calcium.

1/2 c. butter (one cube)
   room temp.
3/4 c. honey
1 egg
1 tsp. pure almond extract
1 1/2 c. whole-wheat flour
1 1/2 c. rolled oats

2 tsp. cinnamon
1 tsp. nutmeg
1/4 tsp. cloves
1/2 cup chopped almonds
1 tsp. baking soda
1/2 tsp. sea salt

Preheat oven to 375°

Blend butter and honey until smooth. Blend in eggs and extract. Combine flour, spices, and salt, and add to wet ingredients. Mix in oats, then almonds until evenly blended. Drop cookie dough onto a lightly greased cookie sheet and bake 8-12 minutes or until lightly browned on top. Makes approximately 2 1/2 dozen cookies.

Ginger Cookies

Spicy and snappy! Molasses give you calcium, niacin, and thiamin.

1/2 c. butter (one cube)
room temp.
1 c. unsulfured light molasses
3 c. whole-wheat pastry flour

1 1/2 tsp. sea salt
1/2 tsp. baking soda
1 tbsp. powdered ginger

Preheat oven to 400°

Blend butter and molasses until smooth. In a separate bowl combine dry ingredients. Gradually add dry ingredients to wet, beating well after each addition until dough is creamy. Dough should be thick, but not stiff. Drop small amounts of dough onto a well-greased cookie sheet. Cookies will double in size, so space apart accordingly. Bake 10-12 minutes or until edges of cookies turn darker brown. Makes approximately 4 1/2 dozen cookies.

Flaky Pie-Crust Cookies

I have some wonderful "sweet" memories of my grandma's pies. Part of the charm of her pies was the fact that there was always some leftover dough to be shaped and baked. Instead of waiting until the next time you make a pie, treat yourself now. These cookies are great plain, or topped with honey and cinnamon, jam, or even cheese.

1 c. unbleached white flour
1 c. whole-wheat pastry flour
3/4 tsp. sea salt
1/2 c. cold butter (one cube)
    cut into small pieces

1/4 c. (or a little more)
    cold water

Preheat oven to 375°

Mix together flours, salt, and butter pieces with a pastry blender or two forks until butter is evenly distributed and flour resembles coarse meal. Add water a little at a time, using only enough so dough holds together and cleans side of bowl. Dough should be moist and workable. Roll dough out on a lightly floured cutting board or counter top. Make cookies as thick as you like. (I prefer the thickness of a pie crust.) Cut into shapes using your favorite cookie cutters, or by hand. Place on an ungreased cookie sheet and bake 17-20 minutes, or until lightly browned on top and darker around edges.

Toppings

Honey and cinnamon: Brush a small amount of honey on top of cookie and add a sprinkle of cinnamon.

Jam: Spread a small amount of jam on top.

Cheese: Even cheese is a great complement to these cookies. Remember that great combination of apple pie and cheese? How about freshly sliced apples, cheese, and cookies?

You can also use these cookies as Christmas tree ornaments. Make small holes in the cookies before baking, let them cool, and string them on your tree with ribbon.

Cake-like Carob-Chip Cookies

Chuck full of carob chips. Calcium, phosphorus, potassium, and some protein are found in the carob chips.

1 c. unbleached white flour	3/4 c. fructose
1 c. whole-wheat pastry flour	1 tsp. pure vanilla extract
1 tsp. baking soda	2 eggs
1/2 tsp. sea salt	2 c. date-sweetened
1 c. butter (two cubes)	carob chips
room temp.	

Preheat oven to 375°

Combine flours, baking soda, and sea salt. Set aside. Blend butter, fructose, and vanilla until smooth and creamy. Add eggs, beating until well blended. Gradually add flour mixture and stir until batter is smooth. Batter should be slightly stiff. Fold in carob chips. Using a teaspoon to measure size, drop onto an ungreased cookie sheet. Bake 9-11 minutes or until lightly browned on top. Makes approximately 3 dozen cookies.

Carob-Chip Bars

Follow the recipe above, omitting 1/2 cup whole-wheat pastry flour. Spread dough onto ungreased 9" x 13" cookie sheet with sides. Bake 20-25 minutes or until lightly browned and firm on top. Cut into squares while still warm. Makes approximately 24 bars.

5—P.C.

Peanut Butter Cookies

I love peanut butter, especially when it is in a cookie. Peanut butter contains no cholesterol and is high in protein and minerals.

1/2 c. butter (one cube)
    room temp.
3/4 c. crunchy peanut butter
1 c. honey
1 egg
1 tsp. pure vanilla extract
1 c. unbleached white flour
3/4 c. whole-wheat
    pastry flour

1 tsp. baking soda
1 tsp. sea salt (if peanut
    is *un*salted)
1/2 tsp. sea salt (if peanut
    butter is salted)
1/2 c. sesame seeds

Preheat oven to 375°

Blend butter, peanut butter, and honey until smooth. Add egg and vanilla and continue mixing until well blended. In a separate bowl sift white flour, wheat flour, baking soda, and salt. Add dry ingredients to wet a little at a time, mixing well after each addition. Drop dough onto an ungreased cookie sheet using a teaspoon to measure size. Sprinkle with sesame seeds and bake 8-10 minutes or until cookies are lightly browned on top. Makes approximately 2 1/2 dozen cookies.

Ricotta Cloud Cookies

In between the taste and texture of cheesecake and shortbread. Perfect complement with tea or coffee. Contains linoleic acid and some protein.

1 c. ricotta cheese
1/2 c. butter (one cube)
   room temp.
1 c. fructose
1 tsp. pure vanilla extract
3 eggs

2 c. unbleached white flour
1 tsp. baking powder
1/2 tsp. baking soda
1 tsp. cream of tartar
1/4 tsp. sea salt

Preheat oven to 375°

Blend ricotta cheese, butter, and fructose until smooth and creamy. Add eggs, vanilla, and cream of tartar, continuing to blend until batter is light and fluffy. In a separate bowl, sift together flour, baking powder, baking soda, and salt. Add dry ingredients to wet and beat until well blended. Batter will be smooth and creamy. Drop a teaspoonful at a time onto an ungreased cookie sheet and bake 12-15 minutes or until lightly browned on top. Makes approximately 2 1/2 dozen cookies.

No-bake Carob Oat Chews

These cookies are quick and easy to make. Think of fudge with lots of oats. Contains protein, fiber, thiamin, and riboflavin.

1 c. butter (two cubes)
1 c. fructose
3 tbsp. unsweetened, roasted
   carob powder

1/2 c. whole milk
1 tsp. pure vanilla extract
1/2 c. crunchy peanut butter
3 1/2 c. rolled oats

Combine butter, fructose, carob powder, and milk and bring to a *rolling boil* over medium flame. Stir continually so that liquid does not burn. Boil *exactly* 1 1/2 minutes. Remove from flame. Add vanilla and peanut butter and stir until peanut butter has melted and is mixed in. Add rolled oats and mix until they are moistened and evenly blended. Using a teaspoon to measure size, drop mixture onto waxed paper. Let cookies cool completely (15-20 minutes). Cover and store in a refrigerator. Makes approximately 3 dozen cookies.

Maple Walnut Cookies

These cookies are very moist and mild. The crunchy walnuts give you protein, fat, thiamin, iron, calcium, phosphorus, plus many more nutrients.

1/2 c. butter (one cube) room temp.	1 tsp. baking soda
1 c. pure maple syrup	1 1/2 tsp. cinnamon
1 egg	1 tsp. nutmeg
1/2 tsp. sea salt	1 c. chopped walnuts
2 1/2 c. whole-wheat pastry flour	

Preheat oven to 375°

Blend butter, maple syrup, and egg. In a separate bowl combine all dry ingredients, making sure that spices are evenly mixed and not at bottom of bowl. Add dry ingredients to wet a little at a time, beating well after each addition until dough is smooth and creamy. Fold in walnuts last. Using a teaspoon, drop dough onto a lightly greased cookie sheet. Bake for 10-12 minutes or until lightly browned on top. Makes approximately 2 1/2 dozen cookies.

Fruity Butter Bars

These fruit bars were so popular at the restaurant that I could hardly keep them in stock. They taste like a pie, but don't look like one. And there's no need to roll out any dough. Some vitamins A and C, plus phosphorus.

1 1/2 c. butter (three cubes]
    Do not use margarine
4 1/2 c. whole-wheat pastry flour
1/2 c. fructose
1 10-oz. jar honey- or fruit-
    sweetened preserves (blueberry,
    raspberry, strawberry, etc.)

1/2 c. unsweetened
    grated coconut

Preheat oven to 375°

Melt butter over low flame. Stir frequently and watch that butter does not brown. Mix butter with flour and fructose till moist and crumbly. Press slightly more than half of mixture onto a 9" x 13" cookie sheet with sides. Spread preserves evenly over pressed dough, leaving about 1/2" margin on all four sides to prevent juice from running over edges. Sprinkle coconut evenly over preserves. Sprinkle remaining flour mixture evenly over top, then gently press down so that dough sticks to preserves and coconut. Bake 20-25 minutes or until lightly browned on top and darker brown around edges. For best results, cut into squares while still warm. Makes approximately 2 dozen bars. Store covered in a cool, dry place.

Almond Squares

These yummy almond treats are rich with protein, potassium, and phosphorus. They are moist with a mild almond flavor, a terrific energy snack and great to take along on a camping trip or hike.

1 1/4 c. butter (2 1/2 cubes)
   room temp.
3/4 c. honey
1 egg
3 c. finely ground almonds*
2 c. whole-wheat pastry
   flour

1 tsp. pure lemon extract
1/2 tsp. sea salt
1/4 c. fructose
1/2 c. unsweetened grated
   coconut

Preheat oven to 375°

Blend butter and honey until smooth and creamy. Beat in egg and extract. Add almonds, flour, and salt and mix until well blended. Spread batter onto a 9" x 13" ungreased cookie sheet with sides. Spread coconut and fructose evenly on top of batter. Bake 20-25 minutes or until lightly browned on top and darker around edges. Cool completely before serving or cookies will crumble. Store covered in a cool, dry place. Makes approximately 2 dozen cookies.

*I use my blender because it's difficult to chop them fine enough any other way.

Date Nut Bars

I love these date bars! They are another restaurant favorite. They are thick with dates and walnuts. Dates are loaded with potassium, iron, vitamins D, B-6, and A, calcium, and phosphorus. Oats are a great high-fiber food and give you added thiamin and riboflavin.

1 1/2 c. butter (three cubes)
3 1/2 c. rolled oats
2 1/2 c. whole-wheat
   pastry flour
1 c. unsweetened grated
   coconut
3/4 tsp. sea salt

1 tbsp. cinnamon
1 1/2 tsp. nutmeg
4 c. chopped and
   pitted dates
1 tbsp. pure vanilla extract
1 1/2 c. water
1 c. chopped walnuts

Preheat oven to 375°

Melt butter over a low flame (avoid browning). While butter is melting, combine oats, flour, coconut, salt, and spices in a separate bowl. Mix well so spices don't settle to bottom of bowl. Add melted butter and mix until moistened. Press half of mixture evenly onto a 9" x 13" cookie sheet with sides and set aside. Cook dates, vanilla, water, and nuts over a medium flame until ingredients thicken (8-10 minutes). Stir occasionally to prevent burning. Spread mixture evenly over pressed oats. Sprinkle remaining oat mixture on top of dates and gently press down so that oats stick to dates. Bake 30-35 minutes or until lightly brown around the edges. Cut into squares while still warm. May be stored in or out of refrigerator in a covered container. Makes approximately 2 dozen bars.

Fresh Apple Date Roll

I like to serve these with brunch because they not only look impressive, they taste impressive! They also give the impression that you have been slaving away in the kitchen instead of sleeping in, when in fact they are easy to prepare.

Preheat oven to 375°

6-oz. cream cheese (room temp).	1/2 tsp. baking soda
1/2 c. butter (one cube) room temp.	1/4 tsp. sea salt
	1 1/2 c. whole-wheat pastry flour

Blend together cream cheese and butter until smooth and creamy. Add baking soda and salt and blend in. Add flour gradually, beating well after each addition. Blend until dough holds together (dough will be stiff but moist). Set aside.

The Filling

1 c. dates (chopped and pitted)	2/3 c. water
1 large pippin apple (peeled, cored, and cut into small pieces)	1 tsp. cinnamon
	2 tsp. pure vanilla extract

Combine dates, apple, and water and cook over medium flame until mixture starts to thicken. Stir occasionally to avoid burning. Add cinnamon and vanilla, then gently mash all ingredients together (do *not* mash until smooth; mixture should be a little lumpy). Set aside. Split dough into two equal pieces. Roll out one piece on a lightly floured cutting board until approximately 14" long, 8" wide, and 1/4" thick. Spread half of date mixture on top of dough, leaving about a 1" margin on all sides. Gently peel up nearest end and gradually roll up dough. Repeat this process with remaining ingredients on second piece of dough. Place both rolls on a cookie sheet and bake 50-55 minutes.

The Topping
2 tbsp. butter

Spread one tablespoonful butter over each Apple Date Roll immediately after removing from oven. Serve warm or cold. Store in a covered container.

MUFFINS AND BREADS

It never failed that for special dinners like Thanksgiving, Easter, and Christmas my mom would whip up a batch of tasty bread or muffins. I have carried on that tradition, except that I no longer wait for a holiday to come around. Often I replace my starch (such as potato/rice) with a fresh, hot muffin or homebaked bread. It has never failed to bring bright smiles at the table. And if there are any leftovers, muffins and bread are great at breakfasttime too!

Cranberry Muffins

One usually remembers cranberries during the winter months, but these muffins are too good to bake only a few months out of the year. Cranberries are high in vitamins A and C.

3/4 c. butter (room temp.)
1/2 c. honey
1 egg
2 tsp. pure vanilla
1/2 tsp. sea salt
1 1/2 c. whole-wheat
   pastry flour

1 1/2 tsp. baking soda
1 tsp. cinnamon
2/3 c. whole fresh
   cranberries
2 heaping tbsp. crushed
   pineapple (fresh
   or canned)

Preheat oven to 350°

Blend butter and honey until smooth and creamy. Beat in egg and vanilla. Add flour, soda, salt, and cinnamon, beating until just blended. (The secret to making good muffins is to not overmix.) Fold in cranberries and pineapple. Pour into paper baking cups set in a muffin tin and bake 18-22 minutes or until center of muffin springs back when lightly touched with finger. Makes 12 muffins. Store in plastic wrap or in a covered container.

Blueberry Buttermilk Muffins

If you like blueberries, you'll love these muffins. They burst with lots of blueberries and are light and moist, with a hint of cinnamon. Blueberries contain vitamins A, B-6, C, and potassium.

1/2 c. butter (one cube) room temp.	1/2 tsp. baking soda
1 c. fructose	1 tsp. cinnamon
2 eggs	2 c. unbleached white flour
2 tsp. pure vanilla extract	2 c. blueberries (fresh or fresh frozen)
1/2 c. buttermilk	
1 1/2 tsp. baking powder	

Preheat oven to 325°

Blend butter and fructose. Add eggs and beat until batter is light and fluffy. Add vanilla. Sift dry ingredients together in a separate bowl, then add dry ingredients to wet and mix until just blended. Stir buttermilk in slowly. Batter should be thick and creamy. Blend blueberries in evenly (avoid crushing). Drop batter by spoonfuls into paper baking cups in a muffin tin, filling 3/4 full. Bake 20-25 minutes, or until lightly browned on top and center of muffin springs back when lightly touched with finger. Store in a covered container. Makes approximately 1 1/2 dozen muffins.

Whole-Wheat/Wheat Germ Muffins

These muffins are light, moist, and high in B vitamins. Enjoy them with breakfast, lunch, dinner, or as a delightful snack.

6 tbsp. butter (room temp.)
1/4 c. honey
2 eggs
2 c. buttermilk
2 c. whole-wheat
   pastry flour

1/2 c. wheat germ
1/4 tsp. sea salt
1 tsp. baking soda

Preheat oven to 375°

Blend butter and honey. Beat in eggs. Combine dry ingredients in a separate bowl. Alternately add dry ingredients and buttermilk to wet ingredients. Blend after each addition. (The secret to making good muffins is to not overmix.)Pour batter into paper baking cups that have been placed in a muffin tin, filling half full. Bake 20-25 minutes or until lightly browned on top and center of muffin bounces back when lightly touched with finger. Store covered in a cool place. Makes approximately 1 1/2 dozen muffins.

Applesauce Oatmeal Raisin Muffins

The applesauce makes these muffins extra moist, while the oats help to add a flaky texture. Applesauce contains vitamin A and potassium.

1/2 c. butter (1 cube)
   room temp.
1/2 c. honey
2 tsp. pure vanilla
   extract
2 eggs
1 c. unsweetened applesauce
1 c. rolled oats

1 c. whole-wheat
   pastry flour
1 1/2 tsp. cinnamon
1 tsp. nutmeg
1/2 tsp. allspice
1 tsp. baking soda
1/2 tsp. sea salt
3/4 c. raisins

Preheat oven to 375°

Blend butter, honey, and vanilla. Add eggs one at a time, blending well after each addition. Mix in applesauce. Combine dry ingredients in a separate bowl. (Be sure spices are evenly mixed and do not settle at bottom of bowl.) Add dry ingredients to wet and mix only until dry batter is wet. Fold in raisins. Drop by spoonfuls into paper baking cups in a muffin tin, filling half full. Bake 12-15 minutes, or until tops of muffins are slightly firm. Store in a covered container. Makes approximately 2 dozen muffins.

Maple Orange Bran Muffins

Bran is an excellent high-fiber food. Alone, bran has little taste, but served in a muffin or bread, it tastes great and adds a flaky texture to the flour.

1/3 c. safflower oil
2 eggs
1/3 c. honey (preferably orange-clover)
1/3 c. pure maple syrup
2 tsp. pure orange extract

1 c. whole-wheat pastry flour
2 c. bran
1/2 tsp. sea salt
1 1/4 c. buttermilk
1 1/2 tsp. baking soda

Preheat oven to 400°

Blend oil, eggs, honey, maple syrup, and extract until mixture is light and lemon colored and oil does not separate. Combine flour, bran, salt, and baking soda in a separate bowl. Add dry ingredients to wet and mix together. Pour buttermilk in slowly and mix only until batter is just blended. Spoon batter into paper baking cups placed in a muffin tin, filling half way. Bake 12-15 minutes or until tops of muffins are slightly firm. Store in covered container in or out of refrigerator. Makes approximately 1 1/2 dozen muffins.

Variation
1 c. raisins
1/3 c. unsulfured molasses

Omit orange extract and substitute molasses for maple syrup, then follow recipe above. Fold in raisins after adding buttermilk.

Pecan Breakfast Loaf

This is a very dense bread. Toasting (thin slices) enhances the pecan taste. It's especially tasty when topped with butter or cream cheese. Pecans burst with vitamin A, thiamin, phosphorus, and potassium.

1/4 c. butter (1/2 cube) room temp.	1 1/2 tsp. baking soda
1/2 c. honey	1/2 tsp. sea salt
1 egg	1 c. whole milk
2 c. whole-wheat pastry flour	1 c. chopped pecans

Preheat oven to 350°

Blend butter and honey until smooth. Beat in egg. Add flour, baking soda, and salt. Pour milk in gradually, blending well after each addition. Fold in pecans last. Pour batter into a 9" x 5" loaf pan that is buttered and floured. Bake 35-40 minutes or until lightly browned on top and a toothpick inserted in center of bread comes out clean. Store in tightly sealed plastic wrap. Slice, toast, and top with favorite spread.

Cornbread

In spite of Mike's* all-time sweet tooth, he loves this cornbread. I still make it for him from time to time. Cornmeal is packed with all kinds of nutrients. In addition, this cornbread is the best I have ever tasted. It is full-flavored, moist, flaky, and the millet adds a slight crunch. Yellow cornmeal is high in vitamins A, B-6, niacin, riboflavin, phosphorus, and potassium. It is tasty enough to eat plain or topped with butter.

1/2 c. safflower oil
1/2 c. honey
2 c. buttermilk
3 eggs
2 2/3 c. cornmeal
1 1/2 c. whole-wheat
    pastry flour

1/3 c. raw millet
1 tsp. baking powder
1 tsp. baking soda
1 tsp. sea salt

Preheat oven to 400°

Blend wet ingredients until oil and buttermilk do not separate. Do not allow honey to stick to bottom of bowl. Add dry ingredients to wet, one at a time, beating well after each addition. Batter will be creamy, but not smooth. Pour into a well-buttered (not oiled) 9" x 13" pan. Bake 25-30 minutes or until lightly browned on top and a toothpick inserted in center of bread comes out clean. Store in a well-sealed container or plastic wrap. May be frozen.

*See Foreward by Mike Farrell.

Banana Nut Bread

Bananas are loaded with potassium, and they contain a surprising amount of protein and vitamin C. In addition to their vitamins, bananas are one of the few fruits that can be eaten even after they look like they're ready for the compost heap! The darker the skin the more flavorful your baking will be. Brown spots on a peeled banana are only sugar spots and can be eaten.

1/2 c. butter (one cube) room temp.	1 3/4 c. whole-wheat pastry flour
1/2 c. honey	1 1/2 tsp. baking soda
2 small bananas (very ripe)	1/2 tsp. sea salt
1 egg	1 c. chopped walnuts

Preheat oven to 350°

Blend butter, honey, and bananas. Beat in egg. Add flour, baking soda, and salt to wet ingredients and mix until batter is smooth and creamy. Fold nuts in last. Pour batter into a buttered and floured 9" x 5" loaf pan. Bake 45-50 minutes or until lightly browned on top and a toothpick inserted in center of bread comes out clean. Store covered in a cool place.

WHEN-YOU'RE-TOO-FULL-FOR-DESSERT DESSERTS!

Carob Mousse

This is an extra light, smooth dessert. Cream contains vitamin A, calcium, phosphorus, and potassium.

1 c. whipping cream	4 medium-size fresh
3 tbsp. honey	strawberries
3 tbsp. butter (room temp.)	with stem intact
1 tsp. pure vanilla	(optional for garnish)
extract	
1 1/2 tbsp. unsweetened,	
roasted carob powder	

Whip cream at high speed with an electric mixer, or vigorously by hand using a wire whisk, until it starts to thicken. Add honey and butter and continue beating until blended. Add vanilla and carob last. Beat only until cream is thick and stiff. Do *not* over beat. Scoop into decorative glasses and garnish with a fresh strawberry. Refrigerate for 2 hours before serving. Serves 4.

Variations

Carob Mint Mousse
Omit vanilla extract and replace with peppermint or spearmint extract. Also omit strawberry garnish and top with a mint leaf.

Carob Coconut Mousse
Add 1/2 c. unsweetened grated coconut when adding vanilla extract and carob.

Carob Banana Mousse
Omit strawberry garnish and replace with fresh sliced bananas. Top with a pinch of cinnamon and nutmeg.

Apple Spice Gelatin

Light, cool, and refreshing, this recipe is easy to prepare, and it's a great way to get your vitamin C.

4 c. unsweetened apple juice
5 tbsp. agar
1 tsp. cinnamon
1/4 tsp. cloves

1/2 c. unsulfured raisins
Fresh whipped cream
(optional for garnish)

Combine and cook all ingredients over medium heat, stirring occasionally until juice boils. Turn down heat and simmer 2 minutes, stirring frequently. Pour juice into decorative glasses and cool in refrigerator until set (approximately 2 1/2 hours). Top with fresh whipped cream when serving. Keep refrigerated. Makes eight 4-oz. servings.

Cool Tropical-Treat Gelatin

Perfect dessert for those hot afternoons after school or a refreshing light dessert after a heavy meal. Lots of vitamin C.

2 c. pineapple-coconut juice
2 c. papaya juice
5 tbsp. agar

1 large banana (or 2
small), ripe, but firm

Combine and cook juices and agar over medium heat, stirring occasionally until juice boils. Turn heat down and simmer 2 minutes, stirring frequently. Pour juice into decorative glasses. Slice banana and float pieces on top of liquid. Refrigerate until firm (approximately 2 1/2 hours).

Topping (optional, but recommended)
1/2 c. whipping cream
1 tbsp. honey
1/2 tsp. nutmeg
8 fresh mint leaves

Whip cream at high speed with an electric mixer, or vigorously by hand using a wire whisk, until it starts to thicken. Add honey and continue whipping until cream is thick and stiff. Do *not* over beat. Scoop a large dollop of fresh whipped cream on top of cooled and set gelatin. Add a pinch of nutmeg and top with a mint leaf. Keep refrigerated. Makes eight 4-oz. servings.

Pam's Fresh Strawberry Parfait

Whenever I eat one of these parfaits, it always reminds of me of the soda shop parfaits that you see in the 50s movies. The layered cream and gelatin are a perfect combination and make a delicious dessert.

Step 1: The Gelatin
> 4 c. apple-strawberry juice
> 5 tbsp. agar

Combine juice and agar and bring to a boil, stirring occasionally. Turn heat down and simmer 2 minutes, stirring frequently. Pour juice into 8 parfait glasses until half full. Refrigerate until firm (approximately 2 1/2 hours).

Step 2: Fresh Whipped Filling
> 2 c. whipping cream
> 1/4 c. honey
> 1 tsp. pure vanilla
>   extract
>
> 1 tbsp. pure strawberry
>   extract
> 5 medium-size fresh
>   strawberries

Remove stems from strawberries and cut in small pieces. Whip cream at high speed with an electric mixer, or vigorously by hand using a wire whisk, until it starts to thicken. Add honey and whip a bit more. Continue to whip cream and slowly add vanilla and strawberry extracts. After cream has become fairly stiff, turn mixer to low speed and gradually add chopped strawberries. Continue whipping for a few moments, then turn mixer back to high speed for 2 seconds. (Avoid getting cream too soft by overwhipping.) *After gelatin has cooled and set,* top with strawberry cream. Garnish each glass with one fresh strawberry, stem attached. Keep refrigerated. Serves eight.

"Slice of the Good Life" Baked Apples

These fresh apples are complemented with lots of walnuts, sunflower seeds, raisins, and oats, and sweetened with maple syrup to give a mild maple flavor. A tasty way to put vitamins A and C in your diet, plus some fiber with iron and phosphorus.

2 large apples (red
   delicious recommended)
2 tsp. fresh lemon juice
1/2 c. rolled oats
2 tbsp. whole-wheat
   pastry flour
1 tsp. cinnamon

2 tbsp. melted butter
1/2 c. chopped walnuts
1/2 c. raisins
1/2 c. raw sunflower seeds
2 1/2 tbsp. pure
   maple syrup

Preheat oven to 350°

Slice and core apples, but do not peel. Place apples evenly into a shallow baking dish. Pour lemon juice over apples. In a separate bowl combine oats, flour, cinnamon, and melted butter. Mix until moistened. Sprinkle mixture over apples. Top with walnuts, raisins, and sunflower seeds. Pour maple syrup evenly over all ingredients. Bake 30 minutes. Serve warm. Serves 4-6.

Hot Brandied Pears
(Nonalcoholic)

This recipes is quick and easy to prepare. Did you know that pears contain potassium? Pears also give you vitamins A and C, plus some calcium and phosphorus.

4 medium-size pears	2 tbsp. honey
1/2 to 3/4 c. water (enough to cover bottom of baking dish)	1 c. fresh whipped cream or vanilla ice cream
2 tsp. brandy extract (nonalcoholic*)	

Preheat oven to 350°

Peel and core pears and cut into thin slices. Place in shallow baking dish. Pour in just enough water to cover bottom of dish. Drizzle honey evenly over pears. Cover dish with foil and bake for 20-25 minutes or until pears are soft and steaming. After removing from oven, pour brandy extract evenly over top. Serve right from oven with fresh whipped cream, or on top of vanilla ice cream. Serves 4.

*Available in health food stores.

Fresh-baked Bananas

This is a super-quick-and-easy dessert. You have probably tried a baked apple. How about a baked banana? It has lots of potassium.

2 large, firm, ripe bananas	1/2 c. fresh whipped cream
4 tsp. butter	or vanilla ice cream
1/2 tsp. cinnamon	(optional, but recommended)
1/4 tsp. nutmeg	

Preheat oven to 375°

Peel bananas and cut in half lengthwise and place on a cookie sheet. Spread one tsp. butter on each banana half and sprinkle spices evenly over all bananas. Bake 5 minutes, or until butter has melted. Top with fresh whipped cream or vanilla ice cream and serve immediately. Serves 4.

How to Make Crêpes and Blintzes

Before I tell you how to create a crêpe or blintz, let me tell you what they are and what their differences are.

Crêpes are paper-thin pancakes. They are amazingly versatile. They can be filled with anything from ice cream to refried beans. They may also be served at any meal. The recipe below is for dessert crêpes. If you would like to use these crêpes for something other than a dessert, simply omit the honey from the recipe.

Blintzes are thicker—halfway between a crêpe and a pancake, but are cooked on one side only and then usually fried. They are served mainly at breakfast or brunch because the blintz filling is usually sweet with cheese and/or fruit.

Although crêpes and blintzes can be successfully frozen (or refrigerated up to 2 1/2 weeks) nothing quite compares to eating them fresh.

Basic Crêpe-Blintz Pancake Recipe

2 c. whole milk
3 eggs
2 tsp. honey

1/2 tsp. sea salt
2 c. whole-wheat pastry flour

Whip the milk, eggs, and honey in a blender. Add salt, then add flour a little at a time, turning blender on and off after each addition. Keep flour from sticking to sides. Let mixture rest about 1/2 an hour in refrigerator. Reblend, then make crêpes or blintzes.

Steps for Making Crêpes and Blintzes

1. Place an eight-inch-round frying pan or crêpe pan (preferably made from well-seasoned cast iron) over a medium heat.

2. Brush pan lightly with butter or oil. Pan is ready when a sprinkle of water bounces around and vanishes.

3. Pour in a small amount of batter (just enough to cover bottom of pan). *Crêpes should be paper thin, blintzes a bit thicker.*

4. Crêpe is ready to turn when tiny holes appear throughout and edges look thin and dry. Lift a small portion of crêpe with a blunt knife to see if cooked side has browned. If so, turn crêpe over.

5. Flip crêpe with fingers (careful, they're hot) or if you are an experienced "flipper," just use a quick flick of your wrist. Blintzes do not need to be flipped. Cook them on one side only, crêpes on both sides. Cook crêpes only a few seconds on flip side (no pun intended).

6. If first few crêpes or blintzes stick to pan, brush lightly again with butter or oil. Keep heat constant and work at an even pace. Pan will season itself after first few crêpes or blintzes, eliminating need to rebutter or reoil.

7. Turn crêpes or blintzes onto a dry towel (a paper towel is fine).

8. Repeat process until all batter is gone.

Extra batter can be safely refrigerated for only a couple days. After that it may taste chalky. Be sure to reblend batter if you let it sit. It is best to use all the batter and freeze or refrigerate leftover crêpes or blintzes.

Carob Cream Crêpe Cake With Fresh Strawberry Sauce

This is a very impressive dessert. The extra time that it takes to prepare is worth the oohs and aahs you will get at serving time. It provides protein and calcium, with vitamins A and C.

18-23 cooked and cooled crêpes
3 1/2 c. whipping cream
3 1/2 tbsp. honey

3 1/2 tbsp. roasted, unsweetened carob powder
2 tsp. pure vanilla extract
2 tbsp. butter (room temp.)

Whip cream at high speed with an electric mixer, or vigorously by hand using a wire whisk, until cream starts to thicken. Add carob powder and honey, continuing to whip until evenly blended. Turn mixer to low, or stop whipping by hand and add vanilla and butter. Turn mixer back up to high or continue beating vigorously until cream is thick and stiff and all ingredients are evenly blended. To assemble cake, place one crêpe on a plate. Spread a thin layer of whipped cream on top of crêpe. Place another crêpe on top of cream and repeat until all crêpes are used. Crêpes must be placed directly on top of each other to keep cake straight. With remaining cream, frost top and sides of cake. Store cake in a covered container in a refrigerator until ready to serve. Top with fresh strawberry sauce.

Fresh Strawberry Sauce
1 pint basket strawberries
1 tbsp. honey
2 tbsp. cold water

Remove stems from strawberries and place in a blender with honey and water. Whip until just blended (sauce should be chunky). Pour sauce over cake slices just before serving. Store extra sauce in a covered container in a refrigerator.

Variations
While building crêpe cake, add fresh sliced fruit of your choice between several crêpes. Try bananas, raspberries, or peaches. Strawberry sauce is then optional.

Cheese and Walnut Blintzes with Fresh Blueberry Sauce

These blintzes are tasty to eat and fun to make. They provide protein, phosphorus, and vitamins A and C.

10 cooked and cooled blintz pancakes	1 tsp. cinnamon
1 c. cottage cheese	1/2 c. minced walnuts
2 c. cream cheese (room temp.)	4 tbsp. honey
	2 tsp. pure vanilla extract
	2 tbsp. butter or margarine

Blend cottage cheese, cream cheese, and honey. Add walnuts, cinnamon, and vanilla, and continue blending. Place a large dollop of mixture on each pancake, fold once, then fold in sides and roll up. Melt butter in a skillet and warm blintzes.

Note: Blintzes can be frozen, but are tastier when eaten fresh.

Fresh Blueberry Sauce
1 1/2 c. fresh or fresh frozen blueberries
2 tbsp. honey
2 tbsp. warm water

Mix honey and water until honey is completely dissolved. Pour sweetened water over blueberries and mash gently. Do *not* mash completely, and leave some of blueberries whole. Pour sauce over blintzes and serve.

LIQUID SWEETS

The following drinks were formulated especially to soothe the soul, to accompany a good book, to help the fireplace warm you, and to assure sweet dreams. And of course, they are also great if you just had oral surgery!

Honey Spice Milk

This soothing cup of milk will help you sleep with lots of sweet dreams. Milk gives you vitamins A and D plus protein and calcium.

1 c. milk
1 1/2 tsp. honey
1/2 tsp. pure vanilla
extract

1 cinnamon stick or
a pinch of ground
cinnamon

Warm milk over medium heat until hot to touch. Add honey and extract and mix until well blended and honey is dissolved. Garnish with cinnamon stick or a pinch of ground cinnamon. Makes one serving.

Hot Carob Milk

I find that carob is much lighter tasting than chocolate. Try the change sometime. I think you'll like it.

1 c. milk
2 tsp. carob powder
(roasted and unsweetened)

2 1/2 tsp honey
1/2 tsp. pure vanilla extract

Combine carob powder, honey, and vanilla and warm over a low heat. Blend until well mixed and all lumps are gone. Add milk slowly, stirring constantly. Turn heat up to medium and continue heating until milk is well blended and hot to touch. Makes one serving.

Almond Essence

The mild almond flavor makes this milk special. The almond adds a natural sweetness of its own. Serve it as an after-dinner drink sometime. Lots of protein, calcium, and vitamins A and D.

1 c. whole milk
1 1/2 tsp. honey

1/2 tsp. pure almond extract

Warm milk until hot to touch. Stir in honey until dissolved, then add extract. Makes one serving.

Cappuccino

The best! Truly a liquid dessert. Vitamins A and D with protein and calcium.

1 c. whole milk	1/4 tsp. pure orange
2 tsp. Pero	extract
1 tsp. carob powder	1/4 c. fresh whipped
(roasted and unsweetened)	cream (for garnish)
1 1/2 tbsp. honey mixed	Pinch of nutmeg,
with 1 tbsp. very hot	cinnamon, and cloves
water	

Warm milk until hot to touch. Turn heat to low. Mix Pero, carob powder, honey-water, and extract in a small bowl until Pero is dissolved and lumps are gone. Add to warmed milk and stir until well blended. Pour into a cup or mug and top with fresh whipped cream and spices. Makes one serving.

Spiced Cider

Spiced cider and the month of December have always gone hand in hand around my house. I love the smell of cider on the stove. Cider contains potassium, calcium, phosphorus, and vitamin C.

1 c. unsweetened	Pinch of cinnamon
apple cider	and cloves
1 tsp. fresh lemon juice	1 cinnamon stick
1 tsp. honey	(optional for garnish)

Combine lemon juice and honey, add to cider, and heat until hot to touch. Stir in spices and pour into cup or mug. Garnish with a cinnamon stick. Makes one serving.

Hot Lemon and Honey

Although best known during sore-throat season, this drink is really a very refreshing change from dairy drinks. Vitamins A and C.

**1 c. very hot water
(just before boiling)**

**3 tbsp. fresh lemon juice
3 tsp. honey**

Pour water into cup or mug. Squeeze in lemon juice, then stir in honey until it dissolves. Make sweeter or more tangy by adding more honey or lemon juice. Makes one serving.